FOR THE LOVE OF TOMORROW

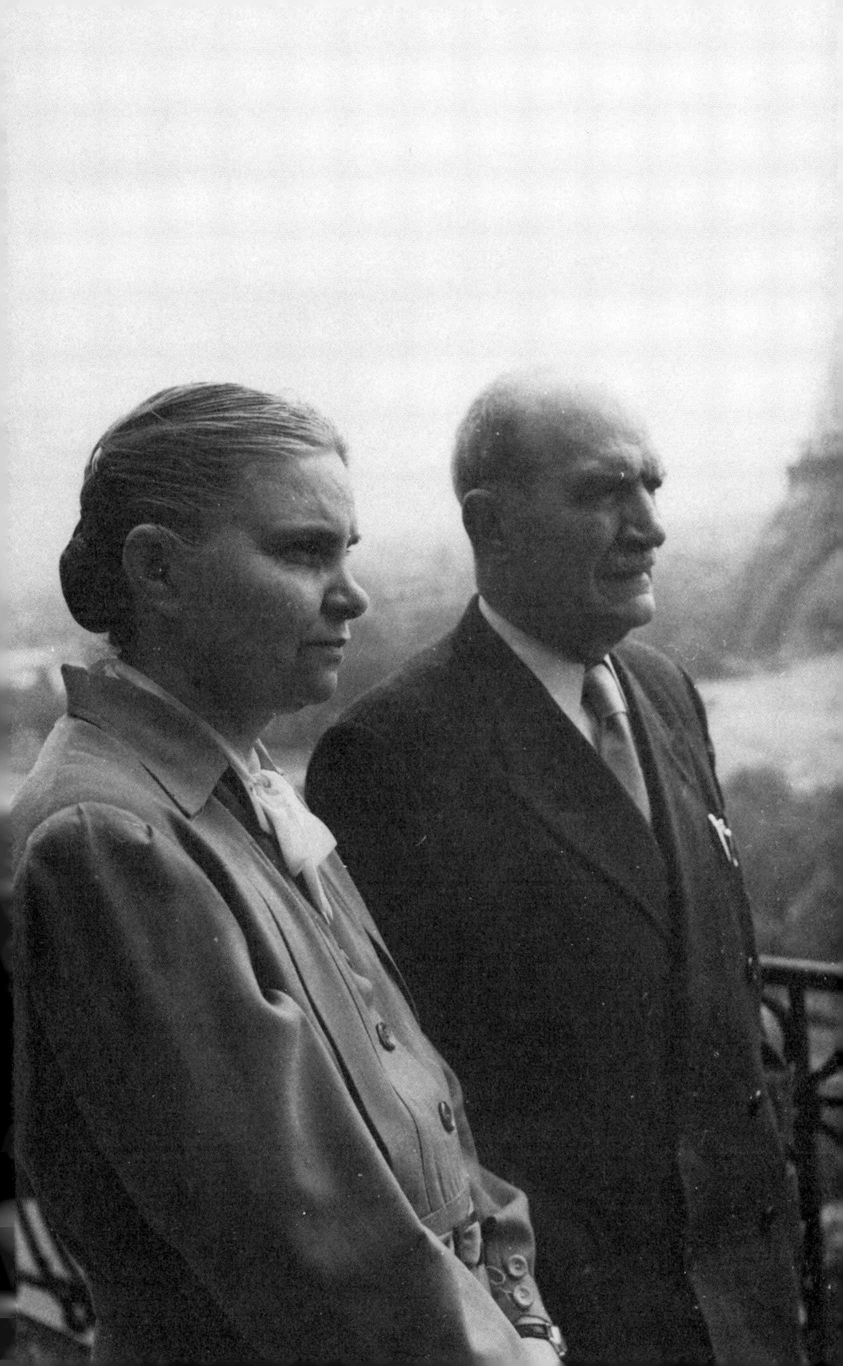

FOR THE LOVE OF TOMORROW

The story of Irène Laure

By Jacqueline Piguet
Translated by Joanna Sciortino

GROSVENOR
LONDON MELBOURNE WELLINGTON RICHMOND VA

Published in French as
Pour l'amour de demain,
Editions de Caux, (Switzerland, 1985)
ISBN 2 88037 015 9

Published December 1985
by Grosvenor Books
54 Lyford Road, London, SW18 3JJ
21 Dorcas Street, South Melbourne, Victoria 3205, Australia
P.O. Box 1834, Wellington, New Zealand.
1103 Sunset Avenue, Richmond, Virginia 23221, USA

© Editions de Caux 1985
© Translation: Joanna Sciortino 1985
Cover design: W Cameron Johnson

ISBN 0 901269 93 X paperback

Photoset in Baskerville, The Good Road Ltd, London
Printed in Great Britain
by Connelly-Manton (Printing) Limited, London

Contents

Resistance	1
Hunger	5
Caux	9
Paris	15
America	21
Le Touquet	27
Roots	31
Victor	39
Germany	43
Berlin	49
The Chapel	55
Calcutta	59
Tunisia	69
Frank	75
Vietnam	81
Mont Valérien	85
An Independent Zaïre	91
Comrade Ima	99
Pretoria	109
Israel	113
Bicentennial	117
Liverpool	123
Spring	127

1940—1944
Resistance

Marching boots shattered the night.

Suddenly the friendly darkness of the Provençal countryside was menacing.

Irène Laure had no time to locate the danger before it was upon her. She was surrounded by a German patrol. A torch blinded her, harsh orders exploded in her ears. She was on her way back from a distant 'maquisard' hideout and knew nobody in the area.

Lost for words, all she could do was point to her nursing kit, an old, black zip-bag. It was always with her on these nocturnal expeditions for the Resistance, as she was in charge of a medical team; and she had dared to hope that it would provide an excuse for breaking the curfew which the occupying Nazis had imposed. It seemed a faint hope now.

'Where's your patient? Go on, get moving!' Her escort did not stand upon ceremony. She was propelled forward by the muzzle of a machine gun in the small of her back and set off blindly towards what might be her death.

Irène Laure was a stranger to fear. But not to anger. Anger had been fermenting inside her since that black day in May 1940 when her son, Louis, burst into the kitchen: 'Mother, the Germans are in Paris!' For a moment she thought she would go out of her mind. Then, in a flash, she knew that come what may, she would never surrender. In that moment, even before it existed, she had joined the Resistance. She little knew that she would draw her whole family after her, right down to tiny Claude, who carried messages in tubes of smuggled aspirin.

But as this starless night dissolved into dawn she had no regrets, not even if her journey was about to end in a burst of machine gun fire.

To the right she could just make out the square shape of a villa. She took a chance and gestured vaguely towards it: 'There it is.'

The soldiers hammered on the door. It was opened by a trembling woman in her dressing gown. Before she was roughly interrupted and driven into the hall, Irène Laure had just time for an aside: 'I told them I was coming to see a patient here...' The woman's eyes flickered. She understood. Without a word, she preceded her 'visitors' upstairs. In a little room where a nightlight was burning lay the grandmother. She was ill and quite obviously so. In frustration and disgust the soldier pushing Irène Laure sent her stumbling towards the bed and she collapsed on to her providential patient.

Few words were exchanged in the villa after the departure of the patrol. Sometimes, looks speak more loudly. At the first glimmer of daylight, Irène Laure made her way home unhindered. She knew that she would resume her perilous expeditions as soon as the need arose, perhaps even that very night.

But danger was not confined to the highways. Sometimes it came right to the door of the ground-floor council flat in Aubagne where the Laure family lived.

One night, Irène Laure woke with a start. Outside there were army trucks, soldiers, dogs.

'This time we've had it,' she thought. Two members of the Resistance were hidden in her cellar and it would not take the dogs a moment to find them. Instinctively, almost without thinking, she grabbed a packet of DDT which had arrived in the last parachute drop, rushed to the entrance of the cellar and scattered a cloud of the powder on to the threshold. The soldiers were already entering the block of flats, dragged by their dogs, who, noses to the ground, were heading straight for the cellar door.

Irène Laure waited, petrified; her bright eyes, steely now, held those of the Germans.

The dogs paused. They sniffed here and there, going vainly round and round in circles. Then, impatient to get outside, they dragged their handlers off on a new trail.

Soon their barking faded into the distance. The night breathed again and the crickets took up their song.

On tiptoe, Irène Laure crept into her children's bedroom. The wide-open eyes of Juliette and Claude shone in the light of her pocket torch. 'Don't worry, everything's all right,' she whispered.

Santine and Paulette, the two eldest girls, were not at home. As for Louis, they never knew where he was, and in times like these it was better not to ask. In a family where resistance was taken for granted, the less one knew the better.

When Irène Laure went back to bed she found Victor, her husband, snoring the snores of the just. Had she been less exhausted she would have chuckled.

The next morning, dustbin innocently in hand, she checked that the coast was clear; Victor discreetly took the two overnight guests on towards the next stage of their mission.

And when the neighbours came round for a gossip: 'What a racket last night! What on earth could it have been?' 'Why, we slept like logs,' said Irène Laure, 'didn't you?'

I know the cost of war. It is always the workers, the children, the women who pay. I have seen the wounded in the hospitals, the dying calling for their mothers. I am a trained nurse.

When the Second World War broke out, everything in me revolted against the Germans. I thought they were a barbaric nation who wanted war, I felt a bitter hatred against the German women. I fought with my whole heart in the Resistance. I was a plague to the Gestapo and thousands of women followed me. I have never been afraid.

I have seen women and children die. Two of my children suffered from decalcification and nearly died. I shall not talk about my eldest son. That is past and needs to be forgotten. We were bombed by the Allies, the Germans, the Italians.

I think of the ruins I have seen – French ruins, German ruins. Whose victory was it? There was no victory; we were all defeated – defeated by evil.

25th May 1944

Hunger

In the spring of 1944 Provence was starving.

On a morning like every other, Irène Laure joined the queue. She waited an hour, two hours, hoping that her turn to be served would come before that fateful, 'No more.'

At long last she reached the counter and into her outstretched hands the shopkeeper placed two sardines. Two. She went home with her shopping basket cruelly light on her arm. She laid the two sardines on the kitchen table and could no longer hold back the tears of despair and exhaustion.

'Oh no, Mother!' exclaimed Santine, 'you mustn't cry. If you cry all the other women will lose heart.'

She did not cry again.

Dry-eyed she heard one or other of her children slipping into the kitchen night after night for a drink of water to drown their hunger pangs.

Dry-eyed, she watched as the decalcification of their bones progressively immobilised Juliette and Claude.

Dry-eyed, she heard that Louis had been arrested; that he had been tortured.

But when the roar of American bombers filled the French sky she rejoiced at the destruction that would rain down on the cities of Germany.

Hunger was becoming acute. For two months a desperate population had been demanding an improvement in the distribution of food. In May, despite rationing, there had been no meat obtainable in Marseilles, no butter and no potatoes. And now, in reprisal for the disappearance of two officers, the occupying authorities were threatening to withdraw the ration cards for bread.

In the market, unable any longer to bear the sight of the ravaged faces of the women of Aubagne, Irène Laure leapt on to a bench and appealed for action—a demonstration for the right to life.

The next morning they set off, a silent river of women. Only women. She had not wanted the men, it would have been too dangerous for them; women by the hundred and children trotting along beside them. Seventeen kilometres of grey asphalt is a long walk, a very long walk on an empty stomach.

In Marseilles, in the Place d'Aix, other processions from Les Carmes, from Saint-Lazare, from Saint-Charles came to swell their ranks. At every crossroads the flood grew.

Into the attractive, sunlit square with its distinguished façades, the Place Saint-Ferréol, poured four thousand women, their silence more formidable than any shouting.

The police on guard duty made no move and Irène Laure went inside the Prefecture* at the head of a little delegation.

They climbed the majestic staircase and without hesitation walked into the Prefect's office.

'Madame,' he thundered, 'what you are doing is dangerous!'

'True, Monsieur le Préfet, but if anything happens to

*Seat of the highest authority in the city, the Prefect, nominated by and representing the central government, at that time subservient to the occupying forces.

me when I get out of here, I wouldn't give much for your skin!'

The Prefect stood up and went to the tall windows overlooking the square. The faces of four thousand women were turned up towards him, and not a sound could be heard.

'You win.'

When Irène Laure emerged between the guards under the massive porch, an eddy in the crowd seemed to swallow her up and she disappeared into the human floodwaters before the police had time to react.

'Now, slip down there, quick,' breathed a voice behind her. 'We're covering you, go on.'

She was gone without a trace. Before she knew it she was in the tram grating its way back to Aubagne.

When she climbed out at her usual stop, she saw to her amazement that the entire population of the town was lining the pavements to meet her. Victor was there, holding Juliette and Claude by the hand. They had been waiting since the morning.

Suddenly the chief of the Aubagne police appeared at her side and two policemen fell into step behind. Arrest. Was this it?

The officer's friendly tone took her by surprise. In little more than a whisper, 'Well, Madame Laure, and how did it go?'

Instantly the tension inside her relaxed. Those few words were enough. They understood one another. Under the protection of this unexpected escort, she reached the workers' flats where the Laures had lived for nearly ten years and where there were only friends, or almost.

Only then, when it was all over, did she realise how certain she had been that this day would be her last in freedom.

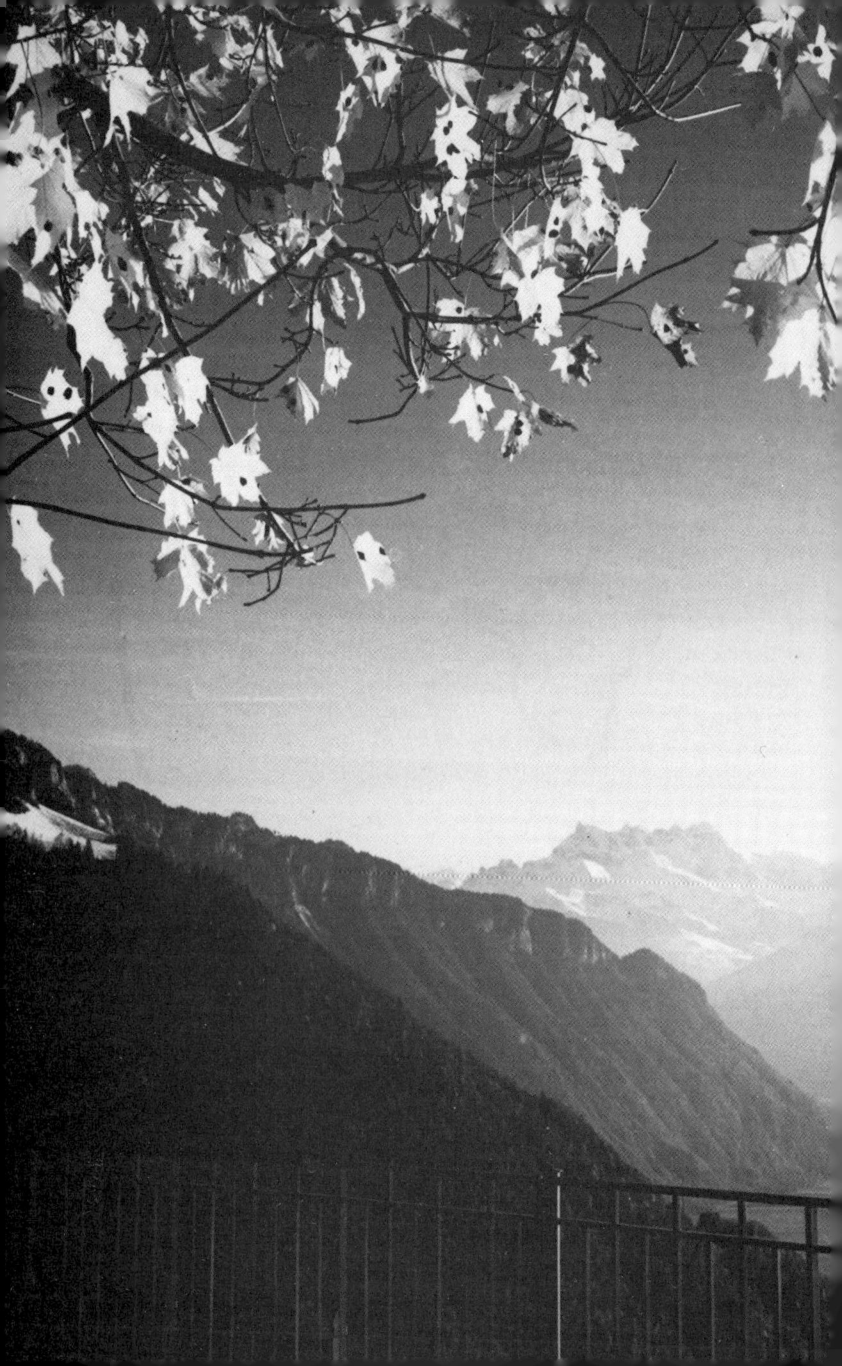

September 1947

Caux

'Never, never. I will never stay under the same roof as Germans. Never.'

All night long she paced round and round her room. Twice, three times, she tried to lie down, but the violence of the struggle within would give her no rest.

From her balcony she looked out at the massive peaks of the Dents du Midi, poised silently against the sky and below, the lake shimmering in a perfect night. But her eyes saw only the tortured bodies of her friends in the Resistance; the little emaciated arms of the children of Marseilles; Juliette, forced by decalcification to spend months in an old pram converted into a stretcher; the unbearable procession of returning deportees for whom she had set up a reception service at the Lutetia Hotel in Paris; and then Louis, her son, her dear devil of a son. She had seen him after his imprisonment—and what they had done to him!

Since her election to the Constituent Assembly as a Socialist for Marseilles, a considerable personal triumph, she had spent herself unstintingly to bind up the wounds of war, both in the House and for the Party. And every attempt made her own heart bleed.

'Madame Laure, you're a Socialist. How can you expect to rebuild Europe if you reject the German people?'

Caux and the Dents du Midi

Through the night she wrestled. What Frank Buchman had said to her that day tortured her. What right did he have to confront her with this dilemma? He must be mad. He arrived from America to lead this Moral Re-Armament conference in the ex-Caux Palace Hotel and he understood not a thing of what Europe had experienced. He could not understand. Did he expect her to betray the starving children, the deportees, her dead comrades, Louis?

And yet, those words ...

He had added nothing. If he had told her to stay on for a few days, she could have argued, explained; merely to hear German spoken made her want to vomit. But that single phrase was like a knife in her side.

Tomorrow, what kind of Europe, what kind of world? As a golden dawn crept over the mountains Irène Laure's thoughts reached out towards a future as yet unborn.

When she emerged from her bedroom, where she had closeted herself without eating since the encounter with Frank Buchman, her eyes were dry and her face impassive. In the long corridor leading to the meeting hall—doubtless not by chance—she met a young woman, half French, half American, Denise Hyde. They had become acquainted in Paris a few months previously and Denise Hyde was one of the people who had spoken to her about the conferences at Caux. In pre-war days Irène Laure had known the work of Frank Buchman but since she had been on the executive committee of the Socialist Party she had had no time for such things.

But then, Caux is in Switzerland and for a French mother in the the summer of 1947, Switzerland meant butter, milk, health for the children. So it was that Irène Laure, Juliette and Claude had been in Caux for two weeks.

'Irène, would you like me to arrange for you to meet a German?'

'Yes.'

'How about lunch today?'

'Yes.'

The two affirmatives were clipped and dry. They clearly did not invite enquiry into the state of Irène Laure's soul. But to Denise Hyde, who was beginning to know her, they spoke volumes.

Punctually at 12.30 Irène Laure was at the door of a dining-room buzzing with the several hundred people participating in the conference.

The German in question was, in fact, a woman. Young, blonde, dressed simply in black, unmistakably an aristocrat. Denise Hyde introduced her. Irène Laure looked straight ahead, her face expressionless. She did not offer her hand.

Without exchanging a word the three women and their translator joined the queue in the self-service dining-room, helped themselves to food and took their trays into the garden. There were tables under the chestnut trees on the terrace. They sat down.

Irène Laure finally broke the silence. The effort made the perspiration stand out on her forehead.

'You represent what I hate most in the world. You cannot imagine what my country has suffered because of you. Our women. Our children, nothing but little skeletons. Our best men killed, tortured. Do you know what my son, Louis, suffered? They tried everything. He never talked. But the state we found him in! He was a wreck, a wreck. And the walking corpses who come back from your camps. I have to receive them at the Lutetia Hotel....'

Impassively the interpreter translated sentence by sentence. The German woman stared unseeing at her plate. Her hands trembled.

Irène Laure spoke for a long time, sifting through her terrible memories of the Resistance. Suddenly she was silent. For the first time she turned to look at the woman she was addressing.

'The reason I am telling you all this, Madame, is that I want to be free of this hate.'

Sunlight played among the leaves. The food was untouched, forgotten. Time stood still.

'I would like to talk to you about myself, if I may,' said the young woman at last. 'My husband was part of the 20th July plot against Hitler. He was arrested. He was hanged. While I was in prison my two children were taken away from our family and put in an orphanage under false names. Now that I have managed to find them again, I am bringing them up as best I can. I realise that we did not resist enough, that we did not resist in time. Because of this you have suffered terribly. Please forgive us.'

There was no let-up in the buzz of conversation at the tables round about. With one accord the four women rose and walked slowly across the lawn to a quiet bench facing the lake and the mountains.

There Irène Laure, militant Socialist in the Marxist tradition, surprised herself by suggesting, 'Perhaps it would help if we prayed together?'

Her prayer consisted of one phrase. 'Oh God, free me from my hate so that we can build a better world for our children.'

Instinctively she leaned across Denise Hyde and laid her hand on the knee of her former enemy.

What I learnt at Caux was how to forgive. That is a huge thing. Because one can die of hatred.

If I had continued as I was, I should have spread hatred right through my own family. My children would have started off hating the Germans, then the bosses and who would have been next?

Hatred, I am afraid, is an incredibly strong force. Unity is also a force.

Isn't it a woman's role, a mother's role (and isn't every woman a mother of mankind?) to maintain the links, to maintain the unity?

November 1947

Paris

'Socialist Women's office, good morning? Yes, just a minute, please... Irène, it's for you. Denise something.'

'Tell her I'm not here. No, on second thoughts, I'll take it.'

Since her tempestuous stay in Caux, Irène Laure had scarcely seen Denise Hyde. At the Cité Malesherbes, headquarters of the Socialist Party (SFIO)*, she did not have a minute to herself.

When she went to Paris at the end of 1945 she was overwhelmed by the size of the task which confronted her. Her office became the crossroads of all the distress of France and the source of countless initiatives. Fired by her example, her secretaries put their backs into the work. When they were not sitting in front of their typewriters they were very likely escorting convoys of pallid children into the healthy air of the mountains.

Over and above her social work she had her job as a Member of Parliament. So little did she expect to be elected that on 21st October 1945, election night, she and Victor had gone to bed early. A bang on the door in the small hours woke them. It was the mayor of Aubagne to announce that in the wake of her Resistance activity Irène Laure had been elected, winning a third seat for the Socialist Party in her Marseilles constituency.

It was the first time women had been able to vote or

*Section Française de l'Internationale Ouvrière

stand for Parliament. Thirty-three were elected to the Constituent Assembly and Irène Laure had great hopes of what they could achieve together for the women and children of France. But confronted with the realities of party demarcation, she quickly found herself out on a limb. Women linking hands across party divisions? No chance.

She made valiant efforts. She presented a project, worked out in committee, enabling mothers to have baby linen at reduced prices; the winter of '45-'46 was cold and clothing coupons tightly rationed. But it was so hard to shift those men in Parliament!

On the executive committee of the Socialist Party, too, she felt hampered, trapped in discussions about doctrine and electoral tactics. 'The people do not understand what we are talking about, and hardship is increasing all the time. They have had enough of suffering and we must act fast, very fast.' Her voice trembled with indignation, but her appeal got no further than the minutes of the meeting.

Her social work, on the other hand, mobilised all her resources. The executive was only too delighted to unload on to her many of its responsibilities in the Red Cross, hospitals, prisons, schools. So it was almost a relief to her not to be re-elected to the second Constituent Assembly in June 1946.

Then came her visit to Caux. On her return she tried to convey to her colleagues the 'Internationale in action' she had seen there, but Cité Malesherbes was haunted by the memory of comrades tortured and liquidated.

She represented France, on the United Nations committee funding aid to children after the war. The prevailing mood was to exclude German children from the allocation of aid. Braving general hostility, she pleaded for them with all the fire that the liberation from her own hatred had given her. Little by little she could see comprehension growing.

'Keep going, keep going,' came a whisper of encouragement. And she kept going, finally demanding a vote in committee. That winter the children of Germany received their American milk, just like the French and the Dutch.

And here was Denise Hyde surfacing again, throwing out a wild suggestion on the telephone. 'Come with me to Richmond, USA, for a Moral Re-Armament conference.'

For a moment words failed her. Was this how she was meant to pursue what she had begun at Caux?

She had surrendered her hatred to a voice inside her pleading for the future. From that agonising moment she had known that she was devoting herself to an immeasurable task of reconciliation which would demand more of her than anything she had ever undertaken.

But America, the bête noire of all her comrades, capitalism incarnate!

She fought off the suggestion vigorously. There were milk distributions, summer camps for children, all the women who depended on her and then, in Aubagne, Victor and her own youngest children with whom she was able to spend so little time and who were expecting her for Christmas.

Denise Hyde did not seem to be impressed so she racked her brains for other arguments. An inspiration! 'I'll have to get Léon Blum's permission.' The perfect parry, she thought. That elder statesman of French Socialism would support her. 'The United States!' exclaimed Léon Blum, 'that's a chance not to be missed! If you want to understand the world, you must get to know America. Go, go.'

'Anyway,' objected Irène Laure, 'it takes six months to get a visa.'

'Not on your life,' retorted Léon Blum. 'You'll see. I'll help you.'

A dumbfounded Irène Laure left Léon Blum with four letters in her black bag: a recommendation to the US Embassy, thanks to which she obtained her visa in two hours, and three introductions to friends of his across the Atlantic.

Their departure was fixed for the following Friday. Denise Hyde, not quite able to believe that it was all arranged, telephoned the Cité Malesherbes on the Monday morning.

'I'm sorry,' answered Odette, the secretary, 'Irène Laure is away. No it's not possible to contact her.'

Tuesday morning, same answer.

Wednesday, again.

And Thursday, likewise.

It was worse than mysterious. It was disquieting.

On Thursday evening, as if it were the most natural thing in the world, Irène Laure telephoned to ask the flight time. Only the next day, after take-off, when seat belts were unfastened, did she drop a little of her habitual reserve.

'You're wondering where I disappeared to all this time, I suppose?'

'Well, yes,' admitted Denise Hyde.

'You see, the situation is such that we could have a civil war at any moment. I don't want my children to be used as hostages to force me to act against my will. That's why I went away. I found someone in Marseilles who will take them to a safe place if it should be necessary.'

She could ensure the safety of her children, who had already borne more than their share of the burden of her responsibilities. But she could not be sure of what would happen to France at a time when the country was rocked by social upheaval.

In ten months of Socialist government the workers had seen a ten per cent reduction in their purchasing power.

The Communist Party, hauled over the coals in September at the meeting of the Comintern, launched a vast campaign of political strikes. In the mining region foremen were held hostage; in the Paris area there were factory sit-ins; striking railwaymen were picketing the trains and blocking supplies to the capital; in Marseilles the supporters of the Communist mayor, who had been defeated in the municipal elections, took the Town Hall by storm and tried to throw the new mayor out of the window. No, without her decision to build for tomorrow and the day after—and the encouragement of that old sage, Léon Blum—she would never have left France in that black period at the end of 1947.

Why did a woman like me become a Marxist? Why do Marxists all over the world fight the class war? Because at one point in the history of the working classes there was no chance of winning your place in the sun unless you fought the class war the way we did.

When I was very young I was gripped by the Marxist idea and the class war. To me the only solution seemed to be an almighty attack on the propertied classes of my country – and of the world, because I am a firm believer in internationalism. But through meeting Moral Re-Armament and Frank Buchman I discovered something which for once in world history would arouse the conscience of mankind. That is why I was willing to pay the price of change.

Why are we ready to pay the price of war in lives and money and yet not to pay the price of peace? I ask you this: are you as ready to pay the price of peace today as you were yesterday to pay the price of war? Ask yourself that question this evening, face to face with your own conscience and absolute moral standards. You will have to choose.

December 1947—January 1948
America

Irène Laure spent her first night on the other side of the Atlantic with a Washington family. She retained only one detail of their evening around the fire; as her American hostess talked, she flashed a needle busily to and fro, sewing a patch on to her little boy's dungarees. Irène Laure could not take her eyes off the scene; her image of an America safe from all material worries, a nation of waste and ease, crumbled before her gaze.

The next day General George Marshall was to speak before the Senate Foreign Relations Committee about his plan to send aid to Europe. Someone suggested that Irène Laure might like to be present, thinking she was grateful for America's generosity.

'Of course,' she said, in a voice that was courteous but about as warm as an iceberg, 'that man is out to enslave Europe.'

The Marshall Plan was much on her mind when she landed in the USA. All summer in Paris they had fought over the principle. The blunt refusal from Moscow to allow economic aid for the whole of Europe, East and West, sounded the death knell of European unity and opened the era of the cold war.

Caught between hatred of American imperialism and the near bankruptcy of France, the French Prime Minister, Paul Ramadier, signed but many of his Socialist colleagues could ill forgive him for doing so. Irène Laure was among them.

Throughout the morning she sat motionless in her chair, her eyes on Marshall. In her ear someone whispered a continuous translation of the Senators' questions and the General's answers.

Suddenly Irène Laure turned and fixed her grey gaze on the translator. 'No, I don't think it is true. That man does not want to enslave us.'

She was sharply 'shushed' from all sides but took no notice. For the second time in less than twenty-four hours she had encountered something different from her version of the truth and rather than cling to her own ideas, she was ready to reconsider.

Before taking part in the conference in Richmond, she had still to take up Blum's letters of introduction. One of them took her to the trades union headquarters in New York. A flight of stairs, a maze of corridors, a minute office, a flurry of papers: she might have been back at the Cité Malesherbes!

The little man in shirt sleeves was Levine, whom the two giant unions, the AFL and CIO, had unitedly designated to manage the funds destined to help their brothers in Europe. He acquitted the task with fierce determination, sending off parcels week after week. But, at the mercy of politicking in the French ports, those same parcels sometimes ended up embellished with the hammer and sickle where they had once carried the letters CARE-USA!

Levine had scarcely time to get up from behind his desk before Irène Laure was across the room, her hand outstretched. 'There are children alive in Europe today because of you. My own children are among them. In their name, thank you, you and all our American comrades.'

Moved, Levine considered her for a moment in silence.

'Ma'am,' he said at last, 'I have a constant stream of people of every kind through my office. Until now I have had nothing but requests for aid. You are the first person to come and thank me.'

Then off to Richmond, Virginia, where again Irène Laure found that union of the intimate and the global which had so captivated her at Caux three months earlier.

There were other French people who had come to take part in these exchanges, and one in particular with whom she had little desire to associate.

'Madame, I am paid, and well paid, to keep the workers quiet,' he said.

'And my job, Monsieur, is to see the bosses hanged from the nearest lamp post.'

Humanly speaking, they were nearer to tearing each other's eyes out than to speaking side by side on a platform in Richmond about their hopes for France. However that was just what an American had suggested, no doubt taking his own wishful thinking for reality.

Irène Laure looked thunderous, jaws clenched, eyes glinting. Robert Tilge? The epitome of all she had loathed since her childhood. Not only did he carry the title of 'Representative of the Employers' Association for the North and the Pas de Calais' but he looked the part, with his ample figure that had earned him the nickname 'the elephant' in industrial circles in Northern France. He was a former rugby player and his methods in negotiation were about as persuasive as on the rugby pitch. In short, it was better not to tread on his toes.

However, since meeting in Caux the previous September, they had been aware that beyond their fundamental differences of outlook was one world, a world full of pain and hope. For the love of the people they represented, they finally listened to each other. Then they stepped on to the platform together. Irène Laure was the first to speak.

'All my life I have fought the class war, the war against the bosses. It has always led us into deadlock. I want to continue to fight with all my heart for the good of the working class. I have found in Robert Tilge a heart as big as my own. It is not easy for us to work together, but because we accept the four absolute standards of honesty, purity, unselfishness and love, we are able to understand each other and fight side by side to remake the world.'

Robert Tilge stood for a moment, unable to find words, this man used to producing speeches by the score.

'If someone had told me a year ago that one day I would be speaking beside Madame Laure,' he began at last, 'I would have thought he was mad. I am moved by this outstretched hand because I sense that it is the mark of a friendship that will be frank and loyal. I also realise what great moral courage Madame Laure has in turning her back on the class war and trusting certain elements in management. Many things have separated us. Both of us are going to have to revise our positions and for my part, I shall have to convince a lot of employers that there can be new hope for the country if they are willing to rethink and review the problems of management. Madame Laure and I are entering together what could be the most important battle in the history of France.'

Robert Tilge
Irène Laure

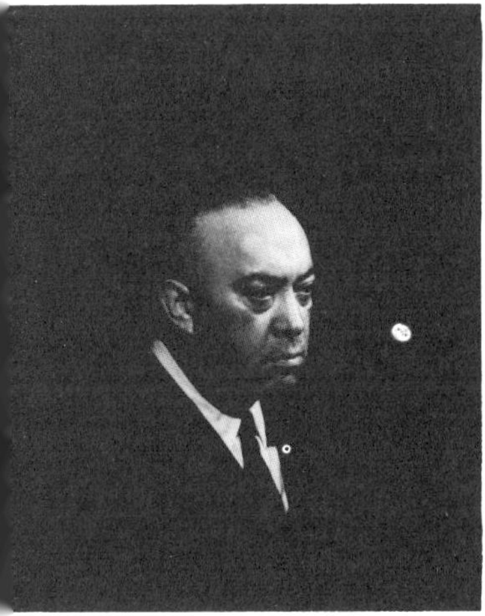

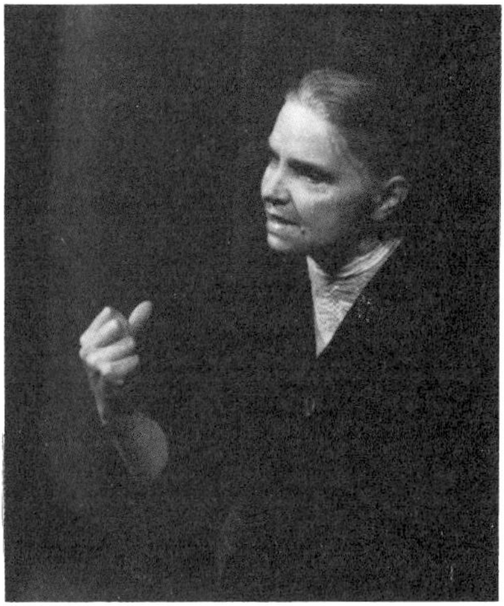

I did not think employers could change. One day I heard a man speak who was my exact opposite. I heard him say, 'I am sorry for my attitude towards the workers. I see that I have served my country badly.' I said to myself, 'If French bosses change, that's quite something!'. I was pleased because I thought this time we had them where we wanted them.

And yet, with all my opinions about employers – and bankers (you don't know the half of what I thought about bankers!) – to be absolutely honest, I had to admit there was a voice in my heart telling me, 'If you changed your own way of looking at things, it might be a good thing for the people of France.' You know, we women are terrors and I was very sure I was right. In the end I had to have it out with this employer, bit by bit. The last step was in America. I told him what I thought of French management and he told me what he thought of Socialism. Well, it wasn't pretty! But today, instead of fighting against each other, we fight together for the good of France. Come and see in the North of France, one of the toughest areas in the country, where we have teams of management and the four major trades unions working together.

I am still a Socialist, I still uphold the interests of the working class. But I have come to understand that the class war of twenty or fifty years ago is no longer necessary and that it is possible to fight for the rights of the workers and win without a bloody revolution. One day classes and class barriers will be abolished and together we can all become workers for a new world.

October—November 1948
Le Touquet

'To transform the social climate of the country' was perhaps rather an ambitious objective.

'It was necessary and so we set about it,' said Irène Laure.

Two people as diametrically opposed to each other as Irène Laure and Robert Tilge, and stubborn to boot, did not learn to pull together overnight.

Clash, hurts, having to abandon cherished ideas—it was as rocky a road for the one as for the other.

Irène Laure had, furthermore, to cope with comrades who considered that she had sold out to the bosses; Robert Tilge with colleagues who accused him of creating a 'God Department' instead of waging war on the new law setting up works councils—which the President of the CGT (Communist-led Trades Union Federation) greeted as 'the final phase before the elimination of the bosses'.

Humanly it was impossible for them to work together. The fact that their teamwork became effective and permanent indicated that the transformation that had taken place in each of them ran little short of the miraculous. In any case, sceptics had to bow to the evidence when serried ranks of management and labour started arriving at the Caux conferences the following summer, 1948.

Irène Laure and Robert Tilge were the first to be

astonished at the response. They scarcely realised the implications of the change in themselves, a change which, from the moment it involved a commitment, was no longer merely a personal matter. In fact they were in the process of introducing into a corrupt social climate an element which short-circuited violent revolution.

Irène Laure then made one of the most difficult decisions of her life and as always, she chose the path that demanded the most of her. To her devastated secretary she dictated seventeen letters of resignation. After years dedicated to her party's struggle, she did not abandon the socialist ideal, but she gave up all her committee work with hospitals, courts, the schools inspectorate and other national and international organisations. It was like amputating a part of herself. And why? Why this sacrifice, initially so misunderstood by her colleagues?

'It was necessary. Absolutely necessary. We must give ourselves totally in order to be effective, and we must spread the message further.'

So a new phase began on the Channel coast amidst the crashing tides of autumn—and the major social conflicts racking France in 1948. To meet the alarming situation Robert Tilge and Irène Laure organised an industrial conference at Le Touquet.

A host of seeming impossibilities were surmounted. The town had been partially destroyed by bomb damage, yet one thousand eight hundred conference participants found lodging. The food situation was desperate, yet there was food for everyone. Delegates from the rival trades union confederations, CGT, CGT-Force Ouvrière and CFTC refused to come in the same railway carriage but they travelled home together. There was no fund to underwrite the considerable costs but people gave what they could. Two hoteliers even waived their bills.

Taking part in the conference were a hundred employers,

three hundred workers, many of whom came in factory delegations, and some sixty miners, together with overmen and engineers, at a time when a major strike in their industry was becoming more and more entrenched.

But these statistics cannot begin to reflect what was launched by the encounters at Le Touquet, which were to affect the social relations of the North of France for a very long time to come.

'For me, personally,' said the Roubaix local secretary for Force Ouvrière, 'Le Touquet made it clear that I am being asked to take part in the creation of a new world.'

Irène Laure and Robert Tilge were in the front line. With an international team they led meetings morning, afternoon and evening.

An employer from Lille said, 'A spirit of team-work in industry is a bomb which pulverises every barrier. On the management side, the barriers are our pride, our selfishness, our mistrust. Our role as bosses means we must make the first step.'

And a foreman in the same company: 'My motto used to be, "It's all the bosses' fault". I have another one now—"Revolution begins with me".'

'It's obvious,' pointed out Robert Tilge, 'that we haven't transformed France in two minutes. But we have already got people accustomed to talking to each other, to discussing things together and we've got them to stop thinking that the man opposite has to be demolished.'

The Tilge-Laure team snowballed. One of the men to join them was Maurice Mercier, National Secretary of the Textile Workers' Federation, Force Ouvrière.

Not least among the repercussions of their work was the signing on 9th June, 1953, of the agreement about procedure for negotiations between the French Textile Industries Association and the Textile Workers' Federations of the CFTC, Force Ouvrière and the CGC, universally recognised as a new formula for labour-management cooperation and a landmark in labour relations. The textile workers gained benefits which the mass of French workers were only to achieve with the agreements reached in May 1969, fifteen years later.

Perhaps it was prophetic when a journalist of the *Voix du Nord* wrote on 13th October, 1948, that the gatherings in Le Touquet created 'a climate, a psychological shock, a state of mind favourable to the discovery and application of solutions'.

But not until the last day of the assembly did Irène Laure realise that the shock wave had reached her own family: a few paces from the grand hall of the Casino, on the melancholy, off-season beach, her sailor husband had signed on for a new voyage.

After Le Touquet: One of eighty textile factory delegations to Caux during the summer of 1951

Born 18th September 1898

Roots

During the war years Irène Laure paid dearly for her love of France. Who would have thought that she had a Piedmontese father, that her mother came from a Swiss village with the delightful name of Vers-chez-les-Blanc (Near-the-Blancs'-house) and that she herself was born in 1898 in Lausanne, where she did all her schooling?

And who would have suspected, seeing her wholehearted defence of the working classes, that she came from a well-to-do family?

Her father was in construction, building a dam here, a cable railway there. Little Irène, her sister and their mother regularly spent their holidays near the sites.

Her parents believed her to be sheltered from the misery of the world, but even as a child she refused to close her eyes. Why were her father's men, working on the construction of the first cable railway from Chamonix to Les Bossons, barefoot inside their boots, even in the snow? Why, when they sat down for the lunch-break, did they only have a hunk of bread and an onion?

The obvious happened. Outraged at being suspected of theft, the Guelpa family cook kept a sharp eye open and little Irène was caught red-handed. She had to admit that the biscuits and the chocolate which were vanishing, the socks disappearing out of Mr. Guelpa's drawer, were her doing. It was her way of re-establishing justice. She admitted it without remorse and enlisted the cook's complicity in continuing her 'social work'.

She took direct action again a little later when the Guelpas moved to Antibes in the South of France; at the age of fifteen, Irène was organising the distribution of milk for illegitimate children and all her pocket money automatically went to help single mothers in Antibes.

Branches of the still youthful Socialist Party were being formed in the area. Irène Guelpa was only sixteen, but if it was a matter of ending exploitation, she knew that was where she belonged. She signed up.

'I won't have it, it's preposterous!' thundered Papa Guelpa. 'What did I do to deserve a daughter like this?'

And Madame Guelpa would reply, resignedly, 'What can we do, she was born like that!'

When war broke out in 1914 she devoted herself to the care of the wounded, whatever her parents' qualms. Four years of hospital life, rubbing shoulders with suffering and death. She came out with a nursing diploma in her pocket and in her heart a fierce determination to fight against poverty and war.

From time to time she lent a hand at the *Café du Commerce* in Antibes, a bar and coffee shop which her father, ingenious businessman that he was, had opened not far from his building site: as good a way as any of retrieving his workers' pay! She knew the hardship that these visits to café brought upon certain families and she did what she could to limit the spending.

One day she flatly refused to give a glass of Pastis to a sailor with a flamboyant moustache, who looked really ill.

'We don't serve alcohol here,' she said.

The violent indignation of the waiter, who served it all day long, and the sailor's fury left her unmoved. She had authority and she was stubborn. So was the sailor, who ostentatiously ordered his drink at the bar across the square.

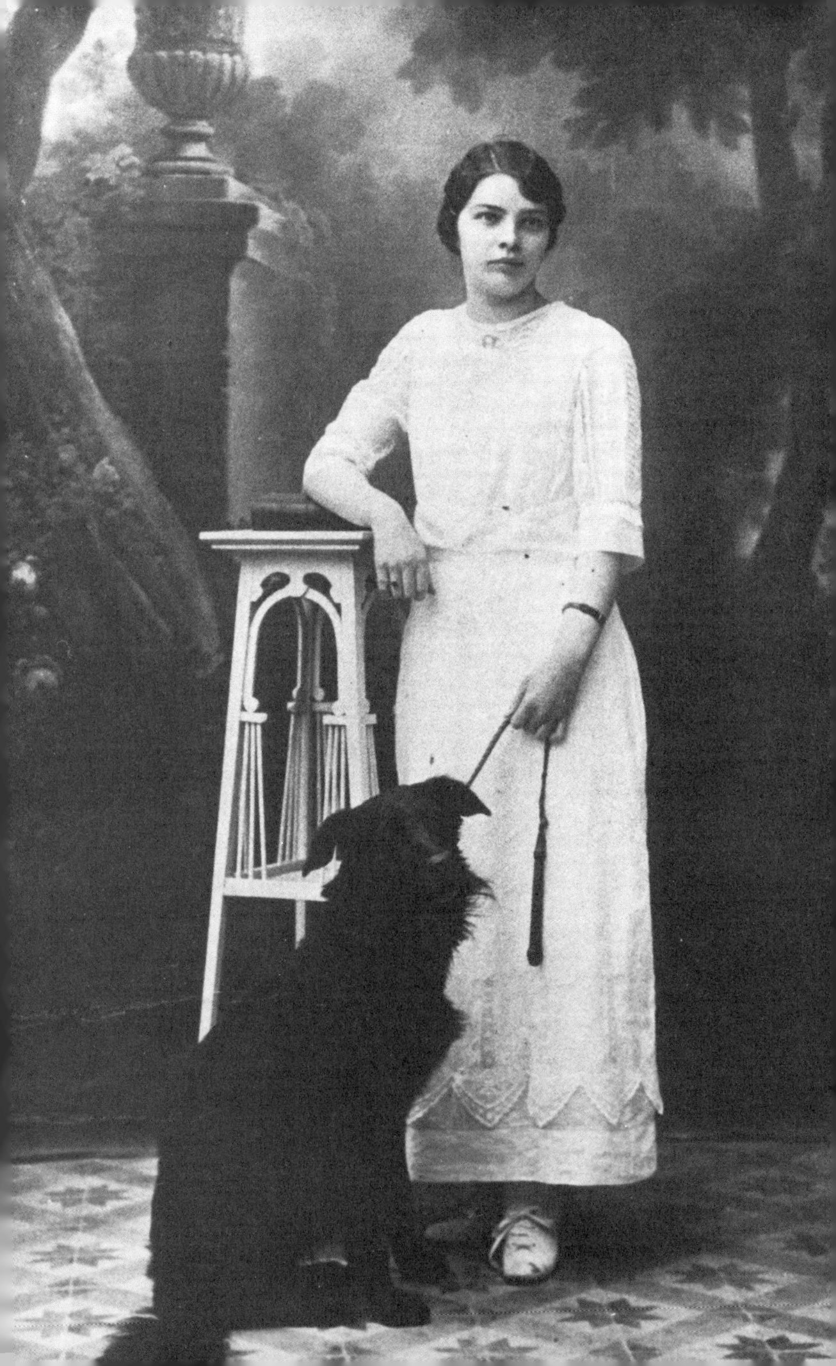

A year later, when she was celebrating her twenty-first birthday, the florist brought her a bouquet of roses, sent by an anonymous admirer: the sailor, Victor Laure, her future husband.

He, too, came from a well-to-do family. His father and grandfather before him had been captains in the merchant navy. He, too, cared passionately for the oppressed. Trained in Marxism by Marcel Cachin, he took out membership of the Socialist Party in 1905, provoking the wrath of his very Catholic family. For years, Victor Laure's sisters passed resolutely on the opposite pavement when they happened to meet him, and once, on a long sea voyage, the Captain, who was a cousin of his, did not exchange a word with him.

So they became husband and wife, married by civil ceremony only, for Victor Laure had rebelled against his Jesuit education, just as he had shaken off the dust of his bourgeois origins. Neither the Guelpa parents nor the Laure parents came to the wedding. Only the sister of the bride and a Laure uncle represented the family.

Instead of a honeymoon they went to the Congress of Tours in December 1920, as delegates of their branch of the SFIO. The split in the Party was pain and grief to them and came near to causing a rupture between the newly-weds, for Victor Laure's instinct, as a disciple of Cachin was to follow him and the majority of the delegates in founding the Communist Party. Then he realised that the conditions imposed by Moscow went against his conscience and, like Irène Laure, he opted for the SFIO and Léon Blum.

Victor Laure had the sea in his blood. It was his life. Despite a brilliant academic record he could never be an officer in the merchant marine because he was colour-blind. But to spend his life on land was inconceivable. Whether as store-keeper, baker or cook in the galley, sail he must. Whenever, that is, anyone would take on a man who had inscribed his name indelibly on the employers' black list by founding a branch of the seamen's union.

For months and sometimes for years at a time, Irène Laure had to earn the family's daily bread, doing night duty at the hospital, sometimes sleeping only four hours a day.

In the morning she would be home just in time to see her little company set out for school: Santine and Paulette, Louis, finally the two little ones, and then the others, because with the Laures, the family was never a closed circle. One day it was an overworked mother bringing the twins she could no longer look after—they stayed a year. Another time it was a friend of Victor Laure's, about to set sail; his wife was in hospital and he did not know what to do with his child.

'Don't worry, Irène'll take care of her.'

And then there was Cousinette, the tiny daughter born prematurely to Irène Laure's sister, who was dangerously ill; Cousinette, whom the doctor had given up for dead, suckled with Louis, a cherished member of the family.

Generosity of heart does not keep accounts and none of the Laures would be able to say with certainty how many children were raised in their home. Nine at least, besides the five Laures.

Neighbours never hesitated to call upon Nurse Laure's services. She was known to be always available for a word of advice, an injection, a bandage—and friendship as well. In exchange came tomatoes, olives or fresh eggs from the hen house.

For the Laures did not remain city-dwellers for long. They moved to Camoins, near Aubagne, to live in the country. So rustic was it that the roots of a fig tree stretched right under the kitchen floor and humped up the tiles. Every summer the whole family went harvesting beans and peas, or picking cherries to make the hundred kilos of jam for the winter 'tartines'.

Often Irène Laure did not know how she would feed her household the next day. But how they celebrated when Victor found a job at sea and the advance on his wages arrived from the company, agreed so that the families of sailors could live until father came home. Of course, the cupboard was stocked with essentials, but Irène Laure dared to splash out too, on a chicken or a packet of really good coffee. The hardships of yesterday and tomorrow were forgotten; it was party time.

When night duty at the hospital was not enough to keep all the little feet in shoe leather, Irène Laure went to town to nurse privately, often to patients in high society.

It was summer and the window of the elegant dwelling stood open. As Irène Laure carefully expelled the air from her syringe, there was a hubbub in the street and a demonstration passed by.

'It's that rabble again!' exclaimed the wife of the patient, angrily shutting the window.

'That rabble is us.'

The sharp retort was instantaneous but perfectly calm. The model nurse was dismantling her syringe.

'Find yourselves another nurse.'

And she was gone. Money never came before her convictions, even if Victor had had no work for two years.

But the pot still had to be replenished and Irène Laure turned from private nursing to attending patients at the thermal resort of Camoins-les-Bains. And so it was that one evening after an exhausting day at the Spa Hotel, as she paused in the corridor to catch her breath, she heard something that intrigued her. It was about changing the world. Whether this encounter with the Oxford Group, which in a few years was to take the name Moral Re-Armament, was chance or destiny, Irène Laure leapt at it.

Socialist that she was, she identified instantly with Frank Buchman's expression of the longing for justice and change. It was like a revitalising draught to her—even if the change in question did have to begin with herself.

Harmony returned to their marriage, which two years of unemployment had charged with tension.

But events were hastened forward. Victor and Irène Laure were involved heart and soul in the Popular Front when the horror of the Spanish Civil War struck. she threw herself into the struggle to rescue Spanish children, collecting money, food and clothing, escorting refugees and organising shelter.

Victor had at last found work again and gone to sea when everything collapsed. It was war. The Nazi Occupation. The Resistance.

In a time of quiet reflection I felt the need to reconsider my life, my Marxist ideas and my hatred of the Germans. I discovered that many things in my life went back to my feelings of aggression towards my father.

At Christmas and Easter my sister and I used to have all the toys and goodies we could ever wish for, but we never had our father with us. And that is where bitterness entered my heart.

As I examined my life, I saw that the roots of my whole being went back to that period of my childhood. No one else can face the truth for us if we don't do it ourselves. It is only possible if we take time in silence to search our hearts. Then we see what we are really like.

Unfortunately I did not have the chance to sort it out with my father because he was dead. But rather than waste time beating my breast I learned to share my experience with others - however difficult that might be - in order that other young people might not make the mistake I made. It is the best thing I can do in memory of my father and mother.

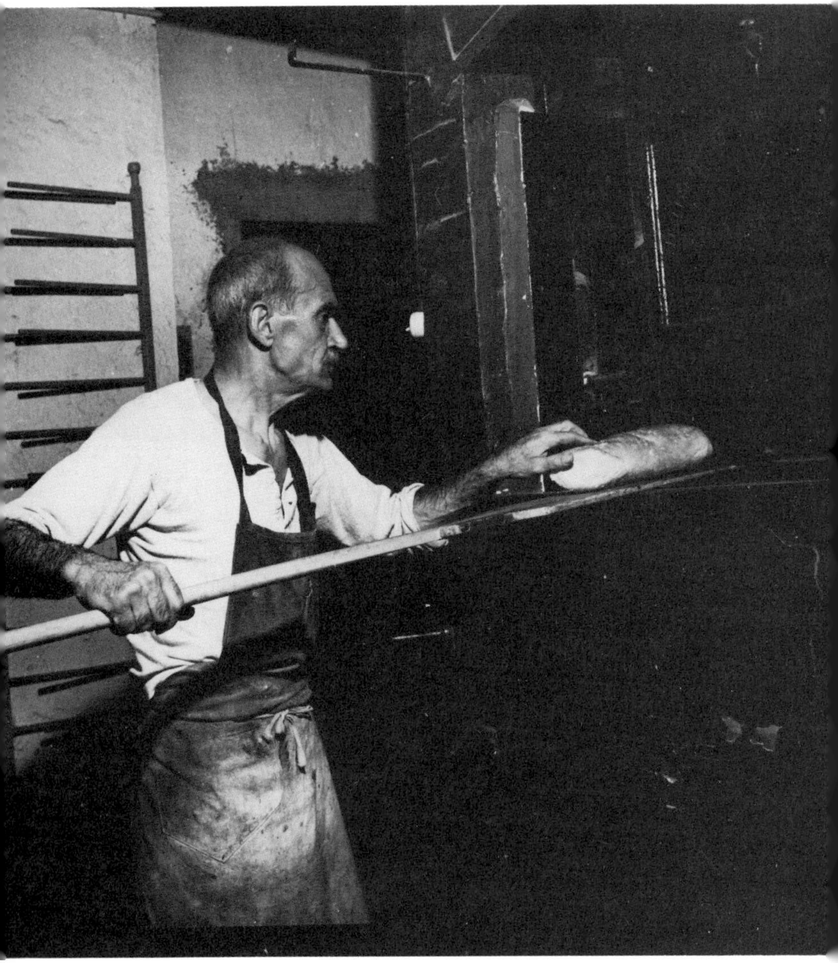

1948

Victor

Victor was silent.

An occasional muttering behind his moustache was all that betrayed his disapproval of this bee in his wife's bonnet by the name of Caux.

His wife had always overworked in the service of others. Since her election she had spent herself at Party headquarters in Paris. What did she need to go off and 'morally re-arm' herself for? Sailor that he was, he still knew how to keep his feet on terra firma and no Utopia was going to seduce him.

That she should have accepted to go to Caux in September 1947, fine: if only to fatten up Claude and Juliette a bit, it was worth the journey. And if by any chance there was some capitalist conspiracy, he knew that his Irène was not a woman to be taken in. She would unmask it.

In fact, Irène Laure did spend her first days at Caux—before the arrival of the Germans—ferreting into every corner. She wanted to know who was behind this international movement and where the money came from. If there was a danger in it for the working classes, she had to know, the better to combat it. She was dumbfounded by an evident sincerity; she was able to go through the accounts with a toothcomb and verify that the people who had made a centre for international conferences out of the former Caux Palace were themselves setting the example in sacrifice. At Caux, the Internationale was not conjugated in the future tense, it was a present reality.

On her return to the family, however, the same spark did not immediately kindle them. On the contrary, her enthusiasm seemed to empty the house. Victor whistled into his moustache and the children melted away.

She resumed her shuttle between Marseilles and the Cité Malesherbes but Victor sensed that the scope of her commitment had grown—as had her hope. There was the trip to the United States and there had been other trips, too.

As the summer of 1948 approached, she began to talk again about the Caux conferences.

'You can go,' he said, 'you can go when you like and how you like. But I'm not going.'

She did not answer, uncertain how to respond.

'You know,' she said a few days later, 'we've done everything together—in the Party, in the Resistance; we've raised the children together. And it's been a struggle. I can't do anything which you are not a part of. I've thought about it a lot in my quiet hour in the mornings. If you don't want to come, I won't go either and that's all right.'

The days passed. One morning Victor was buried in his newspaper, *Le Provençal*. Irène was shelling peas. From behind the paper came a growl: 'All right, I'll go. But just you tell your friends that I don't want to know anything or see anything.'

And so there they were in Caux with Juliette and Claude again, and also with Santine and her little Yves.

Victor spent a lot of time on his balcony, deep in an old wicker armchair. Snow still lingered on the Dents du Midi and the scenery was majestic. But it wasn't the same as the sea.

One evening when Irène Laure was participating in a round table discussion, she saw him out of the corner of her eye slipping into the hall by the far door. Standing, half hidden by a pillar, he listened. She pretended not to have noticed.

'So, does it interest you?' she ventured to ask one morning.

'They're well-intentioned people. But it's Utopia. If God exists he has too much to do to bother with humanity.'

Summer slipped away, a golden autumn arrived, but no enthusiasm alighted on Victor. Nevertheless he followed his wife to Le Touquet in a grey and windy October. Whether because it was by the sea, or because the discussions were all in French and consequently more accessible to him, or because of the natural development of the ideas in his mind, the penny suddenly dropped.

And since his humour was never far beneath the surface, he added, 'We'll black our boots and be on our way!'

Victor Laure, Le Touquet, November 1948

I went out after a meeting feeling confused and wondering if these people were mad.

It was one of those cold, dark November days. Rain, wind, a raging sea. The waves breaking on the beach sounded like thunder.

All around me as I walked along on my own, I saw nothing but destruction, houses gutted and devoid of human life. Such an accumulation of suffering and bitterness.

I measured the immensity of human folly and man's recurring need to destroy and I asked myself: Why? Why? What is the answer, what is the solution? Yes, something must change in the world, but how?

Suddenly I understood that the answer was right beside me. That is why, when Robert Tilge appealed for any who would commit themselves to this struggle to come on to the platform–even though I did not fully understand everything–I felt impelled by an inner force. I was there, alongside the others, to help, in so far as I was able, to rebuild this world.

January—March 1949
Germany

'I had banished you from my heart. I had rejected you from the human race. Forgive me.'

Louis stared at her, horrified. He turned on his heel and left. The door slammed, startling the whole audience. Irène Laure closed her eyes, cut to the quick. Then she began again, the words wrenched out of her. 'I am a French mother. I have suffered as much as you and I beg you for peace between our two peoples.'

For eleven weeks Irène Laure criss-crossed a devastated Germany, Victor by her side like an anchor of certainty when she wavered. Two hundred times she spoke in public, two hundred times she asked forgiveness for having hated.

With her was a varied group of people—a member of the Scandinavian Resistance, Dutch and Canadian employers, English miners, Irish trades unionists, Swiss and, of course, Germans, the ones she had met in Caux.

Essen, Bochum, Cologne, Bonn, Koblenz, Düsseldorf, Stuttgart, Frankfurt, Freiburg, Hanover, Hamburg, Kiel, Bremen. It was like ploughing a vast field.

There were meetings with the governments of the 'Länder' (regions), and with Parliamentary groups, there were press conferences, there were trades union meetings and Socialist women's meetings and radio broadcasts.

To restore Germany to a place in the family of nations

and to inspire the youth with the vision of a future to be built, rather than with dreams of revenge, was no mean undertaking.

All that, Louis could accept. The fact that he had come to join his parents was proof. But to hear his mother apologise, no. That was monstrous.

He had only just arrived when he took the train back to Paris, where he had set up a lucrative import-export business. He wanted to forget.

But he was a big-hearted man. He could not forget.

'Go and open up, Irène,' said Victor in a sleepy voice, 'someone's knocking.' Five a.m. and the chill in the little hotel room was penetrating.

It was Louis. After four weeks without a sign of life, he had come back. He had finally understood what his parents were doing and he wanted to have a part. Across the fat, German quilt which had so astonished Victor, Louis talked for hours. He revealed to his parents all he had done, all that he was. This son, who from the age of sixteen had gone his own way outside the home, was now asking their help to put order into his life (and even into his taxes). He was a new man.

On this particular evening there was no public meeting, no discussion in smoke-filled café. Instead Victor and Irène Laure knocked at the door of a little house in the suburbs of Cologne.

Hans Böckler—already in pyjamas, but what did that matter?—welcomed the comrades Laure with open arms.

It was cosily warm in the kitchen and in a twinkling Mrs Böckler had poured cups of scalding coffee. The shy girl who joined them could not take her eyes off Irène Laure. Given a home by the Böcklers on the death of her parents, she had thrown herself body and soul into the workers' struggle alongside them. She had been doing the secretarial work since Hans Böckler had come out of hiding and taken charge of the trades unions in the British occupied zone. From the following year he was to preside over the whole Confederation of German Trades Unions.

For the moment a query lingered in Hans Böckler's mind. The influential union paper, *Der Bund*, had received and published a copy of an article accusing Moral Re-Armament of having been linked with the Nazis. From the north of Germany to the south, in editors' offices and trades union headquarters, the Laures were to hear this calumny quoted. The article came from a small, political newspaper in St. Gallen, Switzerland and someone had taken the trouble to reprint and distribute it wherever their group was invited.

Victor and Irène Laure were no greenhorns and they knew that although the war of arms might be over the war of ideas was in full swing. It was not difficult for them to re-establish the truth, because a Gestapo publication in 1942 had itself designated Moral Re-Armament as 'the enemy number one' of Nazism. Furthermore, their interpreter, Martin Flütsch, knew the author of the St. Gallen article, who had since been sacked by his paper.

Hans Böckler had already heard Irène Laure speak on several occasions and in diverse circumstances. With the ground thus cleared, he came straight to what was on his mind:

'Whether you are with workers or bosses, you say the same thing. Your message is identical. I can't understand it.

'For me,' said Irène Laure, 'the so-called class war is a struggle for power and not for the greater well-being of the poor and the oppressed.'

How better to explain than by telling him about the social transformations set in motion in France through the transformation in herself and Robert Tilge? So she did, and in detail.

'Yes, I understand,' said a thoughtful Hans Böckler at the end of the evening. 'When people change, the structures of society change and when the structures of society change, people change.'

Outside, the ruins of Cologne stood dark and sinister. But Hans Böckler's eyes were alight.

'See you in Caux, next summer,' said Victor.

'Right.' And an embrace 'à la française' sealed the promise.

Another evening, other surroundings, this time in Düsseldorf. In the hall where Irène Laure and her companions had spoken, conversations were just beginning.

A young man, blonde and solidly built, elbowed his way through the crowd and accosted Irène Laure.

'I was a Nazi. I spent three years in France as a soldier. Then three years as a prisoner of the French. When they released me the only thing I wanted was to go back and find my friends and prepare our revenge in secret. But after this evening, I understand that nothing can be built on hatred.'

Irène Laure was silent, her thoughts in tumult.

'I congratulate you on your work,' he continued, 'and I wish you every success.'

'No!' The answer shot back. 'No,' repeated Irène Laure more gently. 'Why just my work? Why shouldn't it be your work?'

Silence.

'Thank you, Madame. You can count on me. I will strive with you unite our two peoples.'

Dear French friends and comrades, workers, employers, intellectuals, I realise I may cause many of you some heartache. But I must tell you that I have paid the price of a united Europe and thereby a united world and world peace.

I went to Germany. I know I may offend many of you. For weeks my heart ached, too, when I spoke in Germany. But I made peace. Our task is to take the first step towards the Germans so that what happened before can never happen again. It is our task, as French people and children of the Revolution. I am a revolutionary, but I cannot be a revolutionary on my own. We must all be revolutionaries if we are to create the kind of world our grandchildren deserve.

Blue-eyed grandchildren, dark-eyed grandchildren – remember, they await your move and with it the promise of a new world.

Speech by Irène Laure at a meeting of 5,000 people in Lille organised by Maurice Mercier, National Secretary of the Textile Workers' Federation, Force Ouvrière (at the microphone).
On the platform, in the front row, from right to left: Egidio Quaglia, National Secretary of the Chemical Workers (CISL), Irene Laure and Robert Tilge.

1941
1945

SOZIALDEMOKRATISCHE
PARTEI
DEUTSCHLANDS
GROSS-BERLIN

April 1949

Berlin

Day and night, foggy or fine, the American transport planes droned over Germany. Since June 24th, 1948, when the Soviets decreed the blockade of Berlin, a plane had landed every three minutes. Eight thousand tonnes made their way in every day, that spring of 1949, and with them the assurance for the Berliners that they would not be abandoned.

Victor and Irène Laure came to help build that airborne bridge of solidarity, and a bridge of reconciliation, too.

They were a transfusion of courage to all they met: Ernest Reuter, whose election as mayor had provoked the wrath of the East; Franz Neumann, a metal worker, who had dared to prevent the incorporation of the Socialist Party into the Communist Party, despite the presence at the meeting of Soviet soldiers with bayonets at the ready; Ernst Scharnowski, newly elected head of the free trades unions of Berlin.

Like so many other Berlin Socialists, these men had suffered Nazi persecutions, but had not despaired. A visit by Socialists from countries with whom Germany had been at war reintegrated them into the family of nations and was overwhelming.

Louis with his parents in Berlin
With Franz Neumann, Chairman of the Berlin Socialist Party

'How can I help you?' asked Scharnowski. He pulled out his wallet and emptied it into Irène Laure's hands. 'It's all I have. Allow me to give it to you.'

As they went on foot from one encounter to another, the Laures were filled with horror.

'It's all smashed, it's all smashed,' repeated Victor in dismay.

For Irène Laure it was not so much the ruins that oppressed her, mile after mile, as the people who haunted them; the families she saw on the steps of the cellars, under the wreckage of the walls. And, amidst the rubble, the hundreds of women who came and went. With their bare hands they did the work of bulldozers; brick after brick, stone after pebble and stone, they piled up the little heaps along what had once been a street. Faded headscarves on their heads, bloodied feet, bloody hands.

'This is what I wanted,' Irène Laure said to herself. 'I, a French mother, wanted this. I willed the destruction of Germany. I rejoiced as the bombers flew overhead.'

She watched those women and was seared with pain and shame.

Someone improvised a little platform out of a few stones —there was no shortage of those. A summons rang out. From all directions the women arrived, gathering in silence under the grey sky, bowed in apprehension of some new disaster.

'Never again,' said Irène Laure to them, 'never again will there be suffering such as this. I swear to you, I swear to you, I swear to you that I will give the rest of my life so that what you are going through will never again be possible in the world.'

Faces lifted towards her, eyes kindled. They did not listen to all the words, they heard her heart.

They would disperse, they would set to work again with their bare hands, seventy-five million cubic metres of

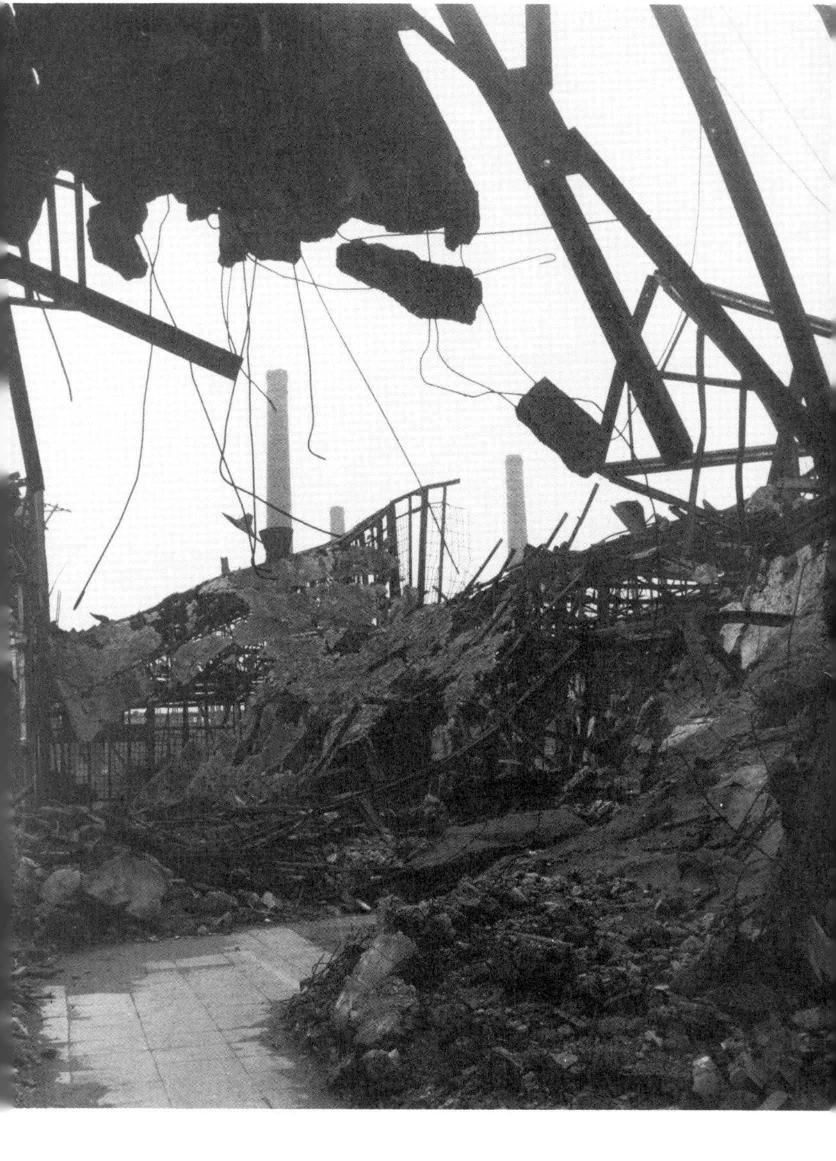

rubble to be carried away. But forgiveness still existed, change was not a fantasy and at the end of the ruins lay new hearts and new homes. They had been given back their dignity.

It was an astonishing encounter. Irène Laure was as marked by it as they. Years later as a grandmother and then as a great-grandmother, if perchance she should weary of the struggle and the highroad, the look in the eyes of the women of Berlin gave her the courage to go on.

Misplaced patriotism, as well as selfishness, fear, rivalry, disillusionment, prejudice and past suffering have divided us.

But must we always look back? Shall we always be afraid?

Division is the mark of our age; will we find the secret of unity?

Between the wars I took in and cared for German children with my own, to try and create solid friendship between children of that generation.

It was all in vain. It is not enough to be kind; we need a common ideology to unite our two peoples. What ideology? The ideology of personal, national and international change.

The world has labelled us hereditary enemies; we can unite and become hereditary friends, who could astonish the world by the strength of their unity.

I am a grandmother and I am fighting for a better world for my grandchildren. I have been a Socialist ever since I first began to reason. Socialism has been my life's ideal. In those days Socialism was able to galvanise the young people of France and bring hope to the world.

As a Socialist I have talked of peace and brotherhood. My great sorrow has been realising that Socialism was neither united nor powerful enough to prevent wars. I had always thought Socialism would bring about world peace.

I tried hard to understand why we had failed to have that unity and power and I blamed the capitalists, the bankers and their entire system. It was they who were responsible for our defeat. I was always aware of their failures, but I never saw ours.

This winter my husband and I spent eleven weeks in Germany. I saw where I myself had responsibilities towards the Germans. Neither my hatred nor my desire to see their cities in ruins had anything to do with Socialism or brotherhood. No nation can ever make war alone, I realised, and I understood my own country's responsibility. For instance, many things might have been different if the Treaty of Versailles had been revised.

Peace must be built on rock. I have sacrificed everything for this idea. I hope my grandchildren will live to see what I was striving for in my twenties, and will rediscover the hope which the dawn of Socialism gave to the world.

1950
The Chapel

That highroad was to take the Laures several times round the world, passing often, in fact very often, beneath the turrets of Mountain House, Caux. There, during the summer of 1950, they met up again with Hans Böckler and many of their new friends from Germany.

The Swiss mountains succeeded at last in seducing the ocean lover—at least a little.

'Yes, everything has to change,' explained Victor dryly. 'The proof? I was a sailor and here I am working as a gardener!'

Every morning he left the bedroom to have a cigarette on the terrace. At least that was what he gave his wife to understand.

'Do you know,' said some well-intentioned lady to her one day, 'I saw your husband at Mass this morning.'

Irène Laure managed not to laugh in the woman's face. She knew her Victor. Forty-five years of militant Marxism and a lively grudge against a Church hand in glove with Capitalism was a bundle not easily dropped.

The next morning Victor Laure took his packet of Gauloises and headed off. Prompted by curiosity or by the shadow of a doubt, Irène Laure followed him. With his measured sailor's gait he walked the length of the building and took the path leading up to the chapel. As if drawn by a magnet she went after him and from the little cloistered porch peered inside. There in the dim light of the nave was her husband, on his knees, his face in his hands. She was thunderstruck. It was impossible, so impossible that she said not a word to a soul.

The days passed. She wanted to talk to him but did not know how to bring up the subject... and to admit that she had spied on him like a jealous woman! The summer drew to a close, the autumn sunsets turning the lake to flame, and Mountain House shut down for the winter.

It was finally in Neuilly, near Paris, where they were staying briefly, that Irène Laure decided to face up to this new situation.

'I need to see a priest,' she said.

Without a query, without a sign of surprise, their hosts summoned Father Finaud, a young priest from the neighbouring parish, who had been a chaplain in the Foreign Legion. Two cups of tea on a dainty tray arrived to ease the encounter.

Irène Laure gave him her confidence. She told him everything from start to finish, the good, the bad—and her Victor.

Father Finaud said nothing. But she knew only too well what he would say in the end and she dreaded it.

'Madame Laure, you must now talk to your husband, because he has to know that you saw him.'

Of course.

But it was not so easy, even for someone whose courage had been tested in the war. It took another two or three days. When she finally brought herself to do it, for the first time in thirty years of marriage she saw tears in Victor's eyes.

'Yes,' he said, 'when I found myself in that little chapel, I had a sort of vision. I felt as if I was being impelled to return to the faith of my fathers. But we didn't get married in church and I didn't dare talk to you about it, because your origins are not Catholic, they're Huguenot. And after all we've been through together.'

'Would you like us to....'

'Should we....'

The question sprang from both sides at once, as always.

And the answer was clear as a bell; if the chapel of the church of St. Matilda in Puteaux had had bells, they would have rung out loud and long on that 23rd November 1950, when Father Finaud blessed the marriage of Irène and Victor Laure.

'It isn't every day that a son of twenty-five witnesses the real marriage of his parents,' commented Louis wryly, after a ceremony as simple as the chapel in which it had taken place.

Thirty years on, five children, two sons-in-law and four grandchildren—a wedding indeed.

The strongest weapon of all is the quiet time. With it we go out to conquer the world. Instead of dropping bombs or firing guns, be quiet and listen. For some it is the voice of God, for others the voice of conscience; but every one of us, man or woman, has the chance to take part in a new world, if we know how to listen in quiet to what is in our own hearts.

March 1953

Calcutta

A lizard, fat and sinuous, slid along the blue wall beside her. Resolutely Irène Laure turned away her eyes.

The heat was frightening. Overhead not even a 'coffee grinder' (as Victor used to call the ceiling fans) to beat the air into illusory coolness. That luxury was unknown in the office of the Hind Mazdoor Sabha, the Federation of Socialist Trades Unions of India, even though in that year of 1953 it could boast a comfortable eight hundred thousand members.

Someone had dug out three chairs for the visitors. On the ground, crammed against each other, sat the thirty leaders of the Bengal sections of the federation.

'And now', said the speaker, 'I am beginning again.'

It was Sibnath Banerjee, the National President, a passionate man and a forceful speaker. Militant in revolutionary movements virtually from the cradle, he was no stranger to underground activity and persecution. In 1922, just out of the Calcutta gaols once again, he left for Moscow, a great hope in his heart and a slender bundle on his shoulder—on foot. A mere six thousand kilometres on carts, goods waggons, the occasional obliging mule and his own sandals. He spent two years in Moscow. He followed Lenin's coffin, bereft as an orphan. Back in Bengal, he took up again the stubborn struggle for the workers of India and for freedom.

Five years had passed since Independence and the fratricidal Partition. A divided Bengal was still in crisis. The prosperous jute industry was cut off from its raw materials, which were on the other side of the newly created frontier. Seven thousand refugees camped on the platforms of the Victorian railway station without water, without hope.

The power struggle was nourished by the misery and resentment that flared up every day into demonstrations and fights. The hammer and sickle blossomed on banners, while Stalin was mourned like a father. A few weeks before, on 8th January 1953, in its programme aimed at India, Radio Moscow had underlined at length the danger to the Indians in the visit of Frank Buchman and his friends, preaching 'Christian love and an end to the class war'.

Sibnath Banerjee was one of those who had called on Frank Buchman's help in the first place. Demonstrating in his own way the team-work which the Indians sought to learn, Buchman had arrived with two hundred people, including Victor and Irène Laure.

'I am beginning again,' announced Sibnath Banerjee to his principal colleagues. 'The Five Year Plan must succeed, or poverty will get even worse. But the Plan is threatened at every level by dishonesty, jealousy and resentment. I am discovering today that it is inside ourselves that we find the cure to these evils. That is the price we shall have to pay to raise the country out of poverty.'

The afternoon was drawing to a close. Irène Laure bowed, hands together, Indian-style, to take her leave, for another appointment awaited her: she had been invited, such are life's surprises, by a family from Marseilles for home-made 'bouillabaisse', a Provençal speciality.

But departure was out of the question. First the guests

must be garlanded. Heavy ropes of multi-coloured flowers were hung around their necks and they then had to sit down again for the no less traditional cup of tea. The cups appeared miraculously and were passed from hand to hand to their destination, followed closely by glistening curry fritters. Solidarity first, said Irène Laure to herself, as she did full justice to what was offered by comrades so impoverished and so generous. There were times when one had to forget that a cholera epidemic was raging in the district and defy the warnings of the medical profession. And as for the 'bouillabaisse', it would just have to simmer for a bit longer.

She was to see Sibnath Banerjee several times at his home in a pitiful street with three little houses standing amongst the other 'dwellings': jute sacking strung over wooden frames.

The Banerjee family's hospitality

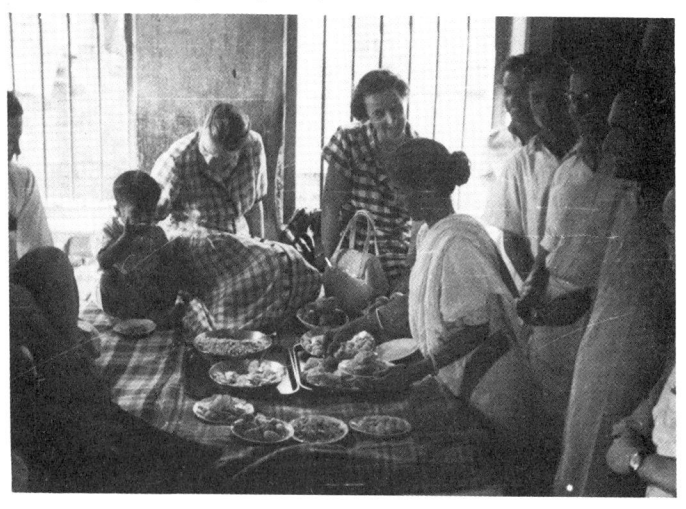

There were fourteen people in the Banerjee family and three rooms in the house. The ninety-two-year-old grandmother opened wide, astonished eyes and the newest grandson, aged two and a half, fingered the visitor's nylon stockings curiously. The main room was at once kitchen, bedroom, sitting-room and office, receiving an uninterrupted stream of union activists coming for instructions or coming to pay their dues.

Already well trained, Victor and Irène Laure left their shoes on the doorstep and sat down cross-legged on the plankbed. A brother-in-law sang a poem by Tagore. Mrs. Banerjee and the daughters of the house passed round sweets made with buffalo milk. Banerjee's colleagues asked questions about the trades union struggle in France, the living conditions of the workers and their leaders. Irène Laure did not sense in them a seeking after power, but an impatience for justice that filled her with anguish: we must not fail them! How childish our fights and how unworthy our demands in the presence of this authentic socialist idealism.

A story sprang to her lips, about the Franco-German unity for which she had so dearly paid herself. She marvelled at the hope which her simple words seemed to give them. Change spreading from person to person moves faster than the dialectic of history, they discovered.

Irène Laure listened, answered, laughed. But the floor was low and the boards so hard. The agonies of cramp made her inwardly beg for release. Ever the practical revolutionary, she took the lesson to heart and from the very next day, first thing out of bed, was doing exercises to limber up her knees.

Delhi and Dacca had just signed an agreement under the terms of which East Pakistan delivered her jute crop in exchange for coal for her industry. In Calcutta the jute factories could function, and just as well, for they enabled hundreds of thousands of workers and their families to survive.

Victor and Irène Laure were invited to visit several of these factories. Amidst indescribable noise and dust they followed the process from the arrival of the bundles of raw jute by boat to the departure of the bales of sacks. From one operation to the next of this titanic chain, the loads were carried by women. They had left their babies in the crèche, a large dark room next to the workshops. Irène Laure was about to be indignant at seeing these naked babies lying on the floor, when she realised that they must certainly be cooler like that than in neat little beds.

Outside the factory buildings, even the blazing sun came as a relief. Three hundred workers were gathered in the courtyard, sitting in the dust. And there were garlands, tea, the same generosity and kindness to touch their hearts yet again. A trades union leader translated into Bengali what the Laures and their companions said.

As everywhere, in the front rows, a flock of little children clustered, their eyes aglow and their mouths wide in astonishment when not in laughter. What excitement when Irène Laure, the better to establish communication, used gestures. 'When I point my finger at my husband, look at these three fingers pointing back at me!' The children vied with one another to point and this simple philosophy of family and social peace seemed to reach them without the intermediary of a translator. Truth to tell, the children were not alone in trying out the new trick and among the leaders of management and labour quite a few fingers were seen to bend and straighten.

'You have brought us illumination,' said a workers' representative. 'I don't know if we shall meet again, but we won't forget that you took the trouble to come from France, Switzerland and Canada to speak to us and to love us.'

If Calcutta is the crucible of the workers' movement it is also the metropolis of wealth.

The opulence, barely minutes by car from the jute factories, was like a slap in the face.

'No, I cannot go in there. Never,' said Irène Laure, her face thunderous.

The monumental portals, flanked by servants in ruby uniforms and plumed turbans, swung open on to a dream world. Fountains, velvet lawns, cool shade beneath the flame-trees. Peacocks strutted, their plumage like fans. The house was a palace.

But Irène Laure did not want to be a princess. She belonged to that other world, the world of the poor wretches she stepped over on the pavement every night, the world of the young beggar—scarcely as old as Paulette's little Christine—whose radiant smile had transfixed her.

To cross that gilded threshold, even for an evening, was that not to identify with the exploiter?

She remembered the management men from the North of France. Those 'haves' who had claimed the right to invest themselves and their possessions in a revolution which she herself had thought reserved for the 'have-nots'. Who was she to deny the rich there that evening the chance to uproot their selfishness?

With tears in her eyes, she went in.

But there were tears in other eyes later, when she declared to her silken and bejewelled audience her belief that they would take up the challenge to change.

Returning to the hotel, exhausted, she stopped for a moment on the poverty-stricken pavement. The sky was rich with stars. Vast as an idea valid for everyone, deep as her resolve to be steadfast to the end, peaceful as promise.

Letter from Srinagar, 10th May 1953

Seeing these masses of poor people, thousands of them, and such desperate poverty, makes me think of the frightful poverty in China, Brazil, in some parts of Europe and all over the world.

It seems to me it is a challenge to our intelligence, to science and modern technology, to all our humanitarian efforts, a challenge to common sense, to Christianity, Buddhism, the Muslims, Jews and Marxists.

I think of the total failure of goodwill alone. When will people put an end to these scandals of selfishness, greed, immorality and fear which paralyse the best of intentions? Who will join us in accepting the challenge to finally upturn the old theories about the world? When fundamental moral change takes place in an individual or a group of individuals, it can quickly turn our needy world into a world of hope and promise, where everyone has a chance to contribute to the good of all. Don't stand on the side-lines. Come and join us!

As Socialists we ought to work for a world where no man goes hungry and no child is without a roof over his head.

We Socialists are by origin and nature internationalist in outlook, or at least we should be. Unfortunately I have to say 'should be' when I think of the last fifty years. We have fought for the interests of the working class in our own countries. We were right to do so, but certainly in France and Italy – and I think it is true of European Socialists in general – we have forgotten our international calling.

We have certainly done good work, because living conditions today are different from what they were in my father's day. But we have failed in our world calling. The kind of poverty I saw in India should not exist in the twentieth century.

Inauguration of the Indian training centre for Moral Re-Armament at Panchgani on 20th January 1968. N G Goray, Chairman of the Indian Praja Socialist Party, and his wife with Irène Laure and Kim Beazley, Australian Labour Member of Parliament.

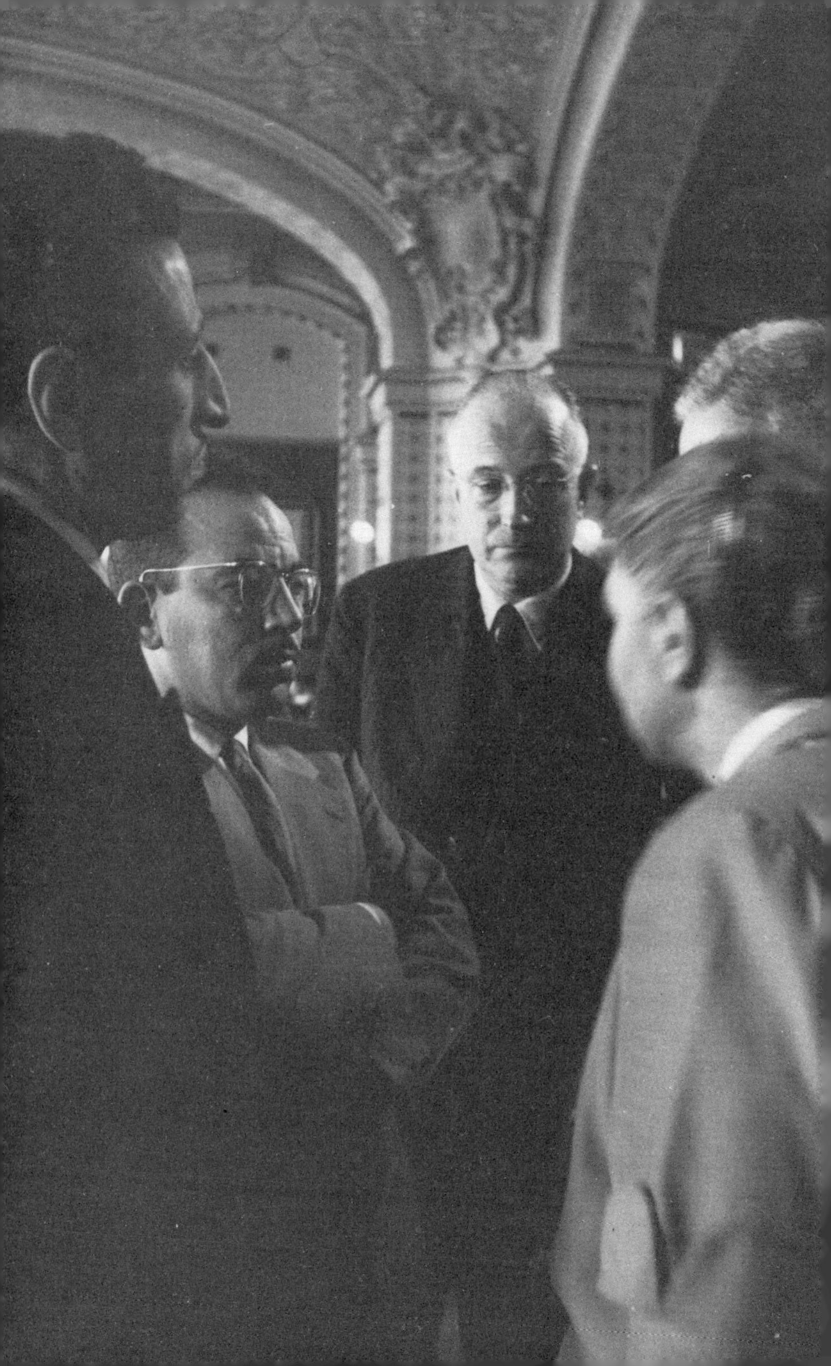

1953-1954
Tunisia

'Oh no, don't ask me to tell my story three times in one day! Everyone's already heard it.'

When she spoke about her change of attitude towards Germany, Irène Laure did it with so much feeling and with such conviction that no one could be unaffected by it. She was often called upon during the sessions at Caux. Those who asked her to speak had sometimes little inkling of what it cost her. If she hesitated it was only for a split second and once she had made up her mind, she gave herself wholly. It was as if it had happened yesterday and she was telling it for the first time.

So that morning in September 1953, many of those listening had heard it before. But for one it was the first time. Irène Laure's simple words had a profound effect on Mohammed Masmoudi.

Tunisia was rocked by violence. Sabotage and assassination were on the increase, repression was becoming harsher. At that time Mohammed Masmoudi was the only one of the leaders of the nationalist movement, the Néo-Destour, not in prison.

When Jean Rous—with whom Irène Laure had sat on the executive committee of the Socialist Party—suggested to him that he might go to Caux, his curiosity was aroused.

M'Barek Si Bekkai, later Prime Minister of Morocco; Mohammed Masmoudi; and Robert Carmichael, French textile industrialist

For months he had been playing hide-and-seek with the French police and the enterprise seemed hazardous.

The customs officials did not ask to see his papers on the French or on the Swiss side of the border. Once over the frontier he began to relax. He even wondered whether to take advantage of this opportunity to go to Cairo or to Libya to join those organising the armed struggle against France from the outside.

Arriving in Caux, he thought he would be faced with well-intentioned people who perceived the problems of his country from afar. But that first morning when he heard Irène Laure speak, his attention was arrested. In 1953, as he well knew, the wounds of war were still open. Could what was happening between French and Germans also be possible between Tunisians and French, who were not as yet divided by such deep feeling?

He talked with Irène Laure of his mother who had written to him from Sousse: 'Today the police came for your brother. I ask God to bless you and to curse the French.'

When he climbed on to the platform on the third morning of his visit, he was a man freed from the desire for revenge and ready to extend a hand of friendship.

'I wrote to my mother to pray for me, but not to curse the French. From this morning I have begun to think that one can adopt a positive attitude even towards those one believes will never change....'

Masmoudi returned without hindrance to Paris, and, through the months which followed, he demonstrated a new openness in his dealings with all the French leaders, from Robert Schuman, then still Foreign Minister, to Pierre Mendès France, who was to become Prime Minister in June after the battle of Diên Biên Phu.

. Meanwhile, on the spot in Tunisia, the situation was becoming more and more tense. In July 1954, without knowing that a few days later Mendès France would drop the bombshell of internal self-government, Victor and Irène Laure were in Tunisia, invited by the Tunisians who had been in Caux the previous summer.

In their meetings with trades unionists, with leaders of the French and the Tunisians, at a press conference, the Laures and their friends strove constantly to build bridges.

The Deputy Director of Education had them meet his superior, a Frenchman, his arch-enemy with whom he had decided to make peace. Less than half an hour after their departure from the offices of the Ministry, there was a burst of gunfire in front of the building and a French officer was killed on the sunlit steps.

One evening they went out of town under police protection to meet some French expatriates, still known as colonials. Victor and Irène Laure had no advice to hand out. All they could share was experience.

'For certain', she said, 'the problems of this country are not only political, they are also moral. Prejudice and mistrust are moral problems which call for a moral solution, whatever the political changes that may be.'

Robert Schuman at Caux

Not long afterwards Robert Schuman was to write to Frank Buchman, 'I know the fine work which you and your friends have done in Tunisia and Morocco. All the difficulties are not yet resolved, but you have been able to create a favourable atmosphere.'

We are just back from Tunisia. There you live all the time with fear in the pit of your stomach. If you go about at night, there are police check-points. The beaches are deserted because everyone is afraid. There we were – a Scotsman, a young man whose grandfather designed the Eiffel Tower, a textile industrialist from the North of France and two difficult Socialists (my husband and myself).

We had meetings with Tunisians, with the Resident General; we had a press conference. I remember, after an evening with some French settlers, one of the most awkward of them, who would not stop arguing about all they had done for Tunisia, eventually said, 'I admit we have sometimes behaved badly.'

We really came to understand the situation in Tunisia and we had to apologise for the attitude of certain French and even members of our government towards this people; because ours is supposed to be the land of freedom; because I value freedom for myself but I also value it for others. If one wants freedom for oneself, one must be ready to give it to others. It is the only way to preserve one's own freedom.

If I had gone to Tunisia before meeting Moral Re-Armament, however full of goodwill or sound judgement I might have been, I should have seen the problem from the French angle only. But now I have a different vision for Tunisia and for France. When one takes responsibility for the world, national selfishness disappears and one has a new perspective.

Victor Laure on French Swiss Radio, 29th August 1959

We have been blind. I have been blind. And this blindness has caused many misunderstandings and some tragedies. I knew it for certain when yesterday in Caux I heard my daughter speak on behalf of the women. I looked at her with bewilderment. She is a woman, she is nearly thirty years old and I had not noticed her growing up.

It is the same blindness that made me see my country the way I wanted to see it rather than the way it was meant to be. It is the same blindness that prevented my country, France, from seeing the evolution taking place in the colonies and that has caused the tragedies in Vietnam, Morocco, Tunisia and the continuing tragedy in Algeria which is an open wound for both our countries.

It is time we pulled ourselves together and tackled the various problems dividing us in a spirit of the most absolute honesty. This blindness, I am convinced, comes from man's being too proud and arrogant to admit that there is a superior power to guide him. It is time we emerged from the darkness and built a new era where there are neither victors nor vanquished but a truly fraternal partnership.

Frank

'Poor Madame Laure, how you've suffered!'

In the immediate aftermath of the war, when she was thrown into turmoil by finding herself under the same roof as Germans, Irène Laure might reasonably have expected to hear such words from any person kindly disposed towards her.

But the sentence which changed the course of her life was in quite a different vein and the person who had the courage to say it won her confidence.

'Madame Laure, as a Socialist, how do you expect to rebuild Europe without the Germans?'

Frank Buchman did not tell her what she should do, but his question was a challenge which shocked her out of herself and made her take responsibility for the future.

In 1949 Irène Laure's new attitude towards Germany and towards management provoked such a storm among her comrades that she felt she was under attack from every quarter at once. There came a moment when she could stand it no longer. She went to see Frank Buchman, who was staying in Caux:

'I'm sorry but that's it. I've had enough, I'm going home. They need me there too. I'll go back to nursing. I think it would be better for everyone.'

Frank Buchman had not a word of sympathy for her, he did not take sides, neither hers nor that of her critics, he gave her no advice. They were silent together. Then he recited four lines of a poem:

'Dare to be a Daniel,
Dare to stand alone,
Dare to have a purpose true,
Dare to make it known.'

For Irène Laure the vitriol seemed suddenly easier to bear.

At the Cité Malesherbes, of course, her association with the 'sharks', the industrialists of the North, was frowned upon and her case was to be brought before the disciplinary committee.

One evening Guy Mollet, General Secretary of the SFIO, recived a phone call. It was Léon Blum from his small house in Jouy-en-Josas, where he was seriously ill:

'If you bring charges against Irène Laure, I will come and defend her. It'll kill me, but I will come.'

Léon Blum did not need to do as he had promised for gradually the opposition abated. Even Jean Courtois, tempestuous secretary of the Socialist Youth, who bitterly regretted Irène Laure's resignation, went to Caux in order to understand better what she was giving her life to.

Frank Buchman was not a greater talker. Nor did he pry. He never asked Victor or Irène Laure about their spiritual life. Besides, he was well aware that a word too many or a word too soon would send them off in a cloud of dust towards their beloved Midi. But he inspired them with his own vision and the size of the challenge drew them relentlessly towards God.

At an engineering factory in Miami

To Louis, too, he proposed the impossible. And Louis did not duck.

It was in Miami. Trade-unionists and management alike from the public transport service had asked Frank Buchman for the help of his team in bringing a new spirit into their company which was in total disarray.

Louis was accompanying his parents. He had closed one chapter of his life and he was searching. The Florida ocean was blue, the beach offered more than one attraction and Louis was no angel. One morning, Frank Buchman summoned him, along with his friends Georges, Armand and Vincent.

'Last night in the quiet,' he said to them, 'the thought came to me that you should go to Brazil.'

The four buccaneers looked at one another, dumbfounded. 'But what'll we do there?'

'Well, when you get to Brazil, drive in a stake here and another there, and string a line between them. When you've done that, hang yourselves on the line like a shirt and let yourselves blow with the wind of the Spirit.'

That was his only advice.

The four emissaries were launched on a crazy undertaking, beside which the adventures of the past were child's play. It proved to be a turning point in their lives.

That was in February 1952. They did not speak Portuguese and they were flat broke.

Perhaps they did manage to catch a gust, because four months later they chartered a plane and brought fifty Brazilians to the United States for a Moral Re-Armament conference: there were delegates from the major trade-union organisations, industrialists, journalists, teachers. For them, it was a new beginning.

In fact with Frank Buchman one was never short of surprises; he expected people to be constantly stretched, instead of putting them into a pigeonhole and labelling them for ever.

One day he needed a message taken to a senior prelate in the Vatican, and he sent for Irène Laure, who refused point blank:

'I'm not the one to go visiting Monsignors!'

'Oh yes, you are.'

'No.'

'Oh yes.'

'No.'

Frank Buchman was stubborn, too. He grabbed his walking stick like the teacher once upon a time:

'Come, come!'

Victor, who well knew his wife's fiery temperament, waited for the explosion and was flabbergasted when Irène Laure collapsed into helpless mirth, followed rapidly by the assembled company.

Irène Laure did visit the Monsignors on that occasion, and even on others.

The adventure of living by faith was one of the many treasures that Frank Buchman shared with the Laure family. He believed that God provides wherever He guides and expected a similar faith from his co-workers. When his close associates had birthdays he used to give them an embroidered handkerchief: a year's salary, he would say with a mischievous grin.

The fact that his work world-wide, endless travel, the purchase and running of the centres like Caux, should have been financed for decades by individuals and often at great personal sacrifice, was surely enough to convince even the most sceptical. For Irène Laure it presented no problems. She found this manner of financing quite natural.

In fact, when she gave up her salaried activities, she was launched without realising it into the nitty gritty of the ideal socialist society: unselfishness and sharing.

In a life of voluntary work, sacrifices are never absent; but neither are gifts. Committing herself alongside Frank Buchman, Irène Laure had, among other things, given up the idea of ever having any home for Victor and the rest of the family other than their ground floor flat on the workers' estate in Aubagne. But....

Landing one day from his vast sub-continent, Louis went to see a friend of the family.

'Monsieur Bronzo, I would like to do something for my parents. I'd like them to have a house of their own and not go on living in a council flat. Can you suggest anything?'

'Well, look here, Louis,' replied Bronzo, 'I've got some property in La Ciotat. Come with me, you can choose the patch you fancy.'

It was undeveloped land, as dry and stony as any self-respecting vine-growing soil; to the east and north, the friendly hills basking in the sun; to the south, just out of sight, Victor's great love, the sea.

Louis laid the foundation stone and on each return from Brazil he came to see how the house had grown, and the plane trees Victor had planted. As for Irène Laure, she had already christened their new home *La Sarine* after a river in Switzerland, an echo of her childhood.

When the blacksmith from Ceyreste came to fit the wrought iron railings for the stairs and the balcony, Victor and Irène Laure, happily impatient, had already moved in. Louis asked for the bill. It was derisory.

'This can't be right,' he said.

'That's my price.'

Then, when everything was finished, the blacksmith explained:

'Now, Monsieur Laure, I'll tell you why I charged you that price. During the war, I was locked up in the prison of Les Baumettes in Marseilles. The fact that I didn't die of starvation is thanks to your mother and what she managed to get in to us behind the iron gates of Les Baumettes.'

So the wrought iron of *La Sarine* is part of the story of freedom as well as the story of faith.

1955
Vietnam

On 5th July 1955, in the bone-shaking bus that linked the airport of Tân Sôn Nhut with Saigon, wise passengers chose the aisle seats. Better to miss the view than to risk a bullet. For, a year after the Geneva Armistice Conference, South Vietnam knew it was only on paper that the fighting had ceased.

The government had invited Victor and Irène Laure and their fifteen companions, all expenses paid, to the Majestic Hotel—which, incidentally, was blown up a fortnight after their departure. The French Embassy, for its part, cold-shouldered them, although they were the first French to be invited by the regime since Diên Biên Phu.

On the morning of the first anniversary of Independence, Irène Laure was preparing to leave the hotel when the porter, already a friend, tried to restrain her.

'You'd better not go out today. It could be dangerous for you.'

'Don't worry about me. I must go. I have to see the President.'

'But you don't realise! See the President today? That's impossible!'

He scarcely believed his own ears later in the morning when he was listening to the radio; the President introduced his guests to the crowd in the Palace gardens, guests from

France, India, Denmark, Africa and Japan; and there was Irène Laure's vibrant voice.

'When I began to speak on the steps of the Palace,' recalled Irène Laure on her return to Europe, 'I didn't know if we would be stoned. Because I'm French, I know all that the Vietnamese have suffered because of us and I can imagine what they were feeling. The most overwhelming thing was that instead of being stoned we were cheered. It showed me how close human hearts are to each other, if we know how to recognise humbly where we have been wrong and start all over again together.'

Victor Laure had a personal link with Vietnam: his father was buried there. Louis-Claude was in command of a ship of the Merchant Marine when it caught fire in the Bay of Saigon. He was able to save all his passengers and the crew and was the last to leave the ship before it went down. He died of his injuries. It was 1902 and Victor was fourteen.

Perhaps the absence of a father goes a little way to explaining the consternation of his mother and sisters when Victor Laure became a Marxist; and such a father, a man who never trifled with honour and tradition and who devotedly every year carried the statue of the Virgin of Notre Dame de la Garde in procession, down into the Old Port of Marseilles.

Victor and Irène Laure stood for a long time in silence in front of the simple tomb of a father who, too soon, had become the hero of a legend. A heavy monsoon sky muffled the day. Past and present merged. The ideas for which people die live on beyond them.

With a last look at the statue of Louis-Claude, Victor and Irène Laure turned away. They were being sought after from every side, by members of the government, refugees from the camps, students, workers' representatives.

A group of trade-unionists was waiting for them. In honour of the French sailor they had brought out the best bottles, but Victor Laure refused.

'Well, you're certainly the first Frenchman I've met who is capable of refusing alcohol!' exclaimed the president. 'What makes you different?'

With a wicked twinkle, Victor began, 'You see, I was a sailor, and when I landed in port, my first visit wasn't to the chapel....'

He had captured his audience and in that little union office, clustered around the empty glasses, they were all ears.

What Victor and Irène Laure were to leave behind them in Vietnam was one of those ideas which can survive storms and even shipwreck.

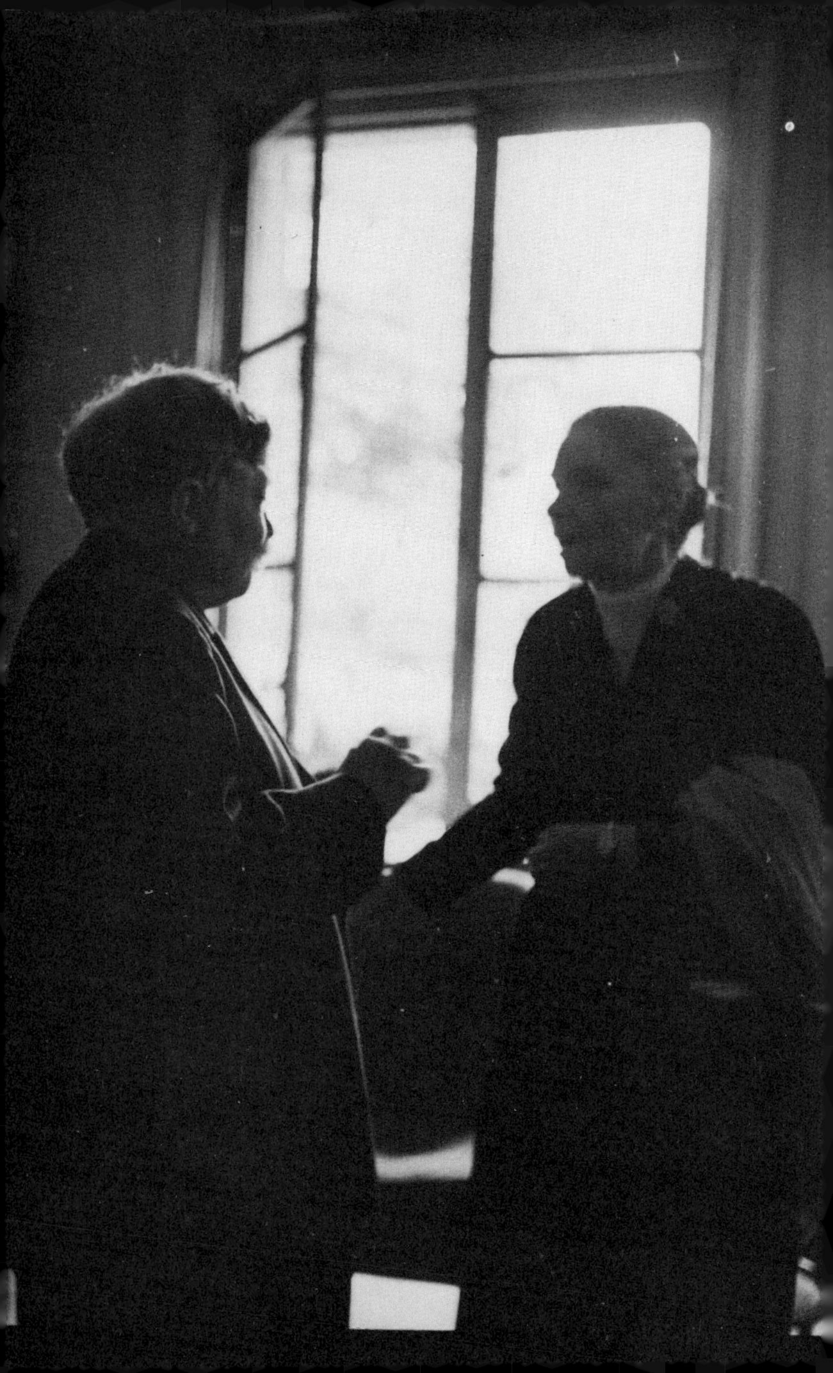

1959
Mont Valérien

'Tell me, Madame Laure, when you apologise, how can you be sure that the other will respond?'

The question was posed with real anguish by Abu Sayeed Chowdhury, President of Bangladesh, exactly a year after his country was born with bloodshed and tears.

'You can never be sure. All that I knew when I asked forgiveness of the Germans for my hatred was that I had to do it.'

No, she had not been sure then. But on this day in 1959 she knew for certain. She saw it before her eyes in the Miners' Social Hall in Lens, Northern France. Ten years had passed since that first visit to Germany, since the first public apology that had cost her such agony.

She stood listening to the Marseillaise, too moved to join in. The people singing were German, miners from the Ruhr in their traditional black uniforms trimmed with silver, and their red-plumed shakos.

One, an underground face-worker, had always wanted to write but his vocation had withered under his wife's sarcasm. Tonight she was beside him on the stage as he presented 'Hope', the play he had written in Caux.

If Irène Laure's heart was thumping, it was not only be-

Gabriel Marcel, Member of the *Institut Français*, who reported the ceremony at Mont Valérien for the *Figaro* of 21st December 1959

cause of this gesture by the Germans but also because their coming to France had given her the chance to co-operate closely with her former colleagues.

It was Guy Mollet's idea that the first performance of 'Hope' should be on the feast of St. Barbara, patron saint of miners: Guy Mollet, Mayor of Arras and Member of Parliament, with whom she had crossed swords at the time of her decisive choices in 1948. A precious ally in all the preparations had been Jean Courtois, the former youth leader, now secretary of the Socialist group in the Assembly. . Several Socialist Members of Parliament and Senators figured on the invitation committee, along with leaders of Force Ouvrière.

As the days and the performances went by—Hénin-Liétard, Puteaux, Paris—the humble and courageous words of the German miners healed wounds and purified the very well-springs of European unity.

On a cold morning of 20th December 1959, Irène Laure walked with them along the paths of a place painful to them all: Mont Valérien.* The miners had asked permission to lay a wreath, as memorial and pledge.

They were the first Germans allowed to enter the fortress. Their guides were the wife of General Paul Ely and Madame Geneviève Anthonioz-de Gaulle, both of whom had escaped alive from the death camps. The crypt was opened specially, its key brought from the Elysée. In a silence charged with emotion they laid their wreath.

Then they walked the uneven paving stones, between black winter trees, to the old chapel where the condemned spent their last night. On the walls were carved their hopes and their farewells, their cries of love and of liberty.

From there onwards, a rough path. Four thousand five

*Hill just outside Paris where members of the Resistance were shot by the occupying forces in World War II, now a national shrine.

hundred men and women had walked that path through many a sorrowful dawn, their feet scattering for the last time the pebbles of the land they had loved better than life itself.

A silent circle closed around the simple red memorial in the clearing. It was here, at the foot of the hillock, that the Resistants were shot.

'We do not ask you to forget, but to forgive,' said one of the Germans. 'We have resolved to dedicate our lives so that such tragedy can never be repeated.'

I am a mother and a grandmother. What happens in the world is the responsibility of us mothers. We bring children into the world and foolishly let others decide their fate. I have a son-in-law who came back from Indo-China seriously wounded. He has three small children. He will come through it – although who knows? My son Claude is a soldier now. If there had not been a cease-fire, he would have gone there too.

How do mothers react to such a hopeless mess? We weep when our sons are taken – and tears never cured anything – instead of creating the climate for a new world. That is our responsibility. So, what are you going to do about safeguarding the future of your children?

Thirty years later, Irène Laure's grand-daughter, Annie, brings a German into the family.

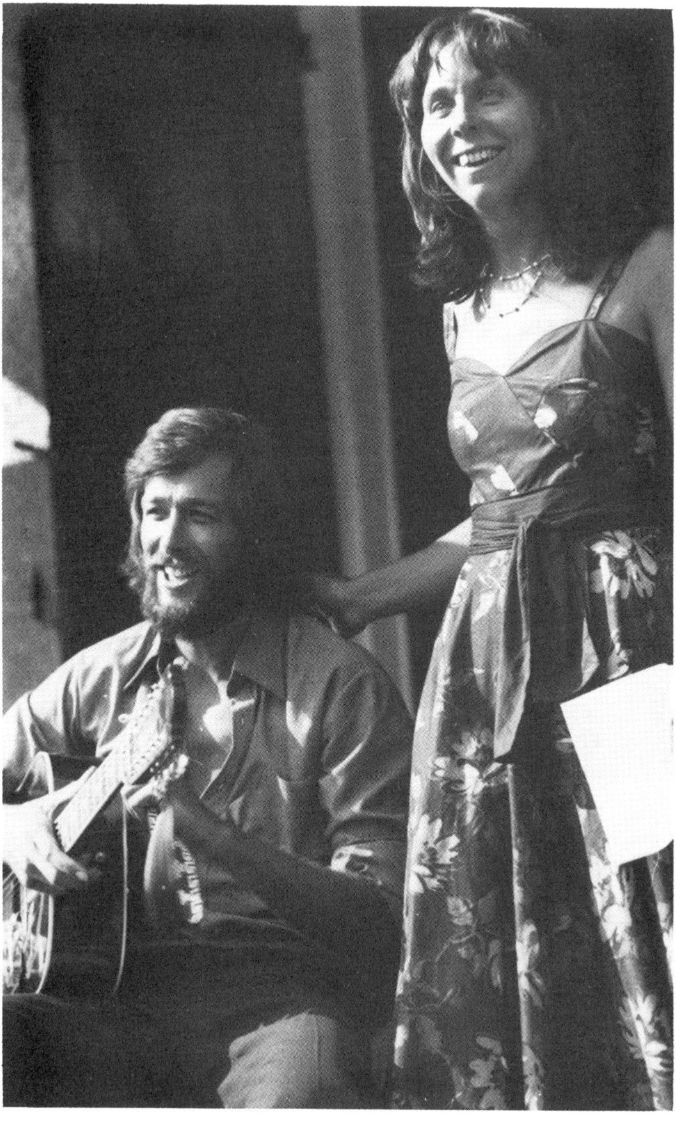

July—August 1960
An Independent Zaïre

An immense red moon stared down at the city.

Since the panic flight of the Europeans towards the Embassies the silence was no longer punctuated by the sound of sporadic shots in the distance, or jeeps careering down Albert I Boulevard.

A dog howled disconsolately and others echoed a mournful response. Perhaps they knew that their abandonment marked the end of an era.

From her eighth floor balcony, Irène Laure pondered the night. It was 7th July, 1960. A fortnight—a century—since she had landed in 'Leo' (Leopoldville), as they called Kinshasa then. The countdown to Independence was drawing to an end and the tension was mounting.

She had been invited by a charming Belgian woman to stay in an exquisite villa near the river and was unpacking when a black man appeared, dressed entirely in white:

'Have you any washing, Madame?'

'No, thank you very much, Monsieur, I have only just arrived.'

'Would you like your shoes polished?'

'Oh no, thank you, I always do that myself.'

Oblivious of the incongruity of her reply and happy to be making her first contact with a native of the country, she embarked on a conversation. A mother and a grandmother before anything else, she asked him about his own family; this man, who looked so young, turned out to have as many grandchildren as she. The sounds of their chatter drew the mistress of the house.

'Run along, Joseph, you've no business here!' she exclaimed, using the familiar 'tu' in addressing him.

And she attempted an explanation to Irène Laure, who was trembling with indignation: it was ridiculous to use the polite 'vous' in talking to a 'Boy', and she must get used to living like the whites who knew the usages and customs of the country.

'But, Madame, I came here at the invitation of the new leaders of the Congo and I will not say 'tu' to a man I do not know, who furthermore is a father and a grandfather.'

A shadow had entered the dream villa and it hung over the few days that Irène Laure remained there before she moved into an apartment in the centre of town, belonging to a family who had returned to Europe.

It was a 'luxury' block, but they had to manage with the little remaining furniture, no household linen and no crockery, as well as waging a fierce battle for possession against armies of cockroaches. Canny housewife that she was, Irène Laure always packed into her little suitcase a carefully cut-out square of one of Victor's old vests for—polishing her shoes. Providential cloth, because, with Independence imminent, the shops were closed for several days and there was nothing else for dusting and cleaning the bathroom or the kitchen.

Excitement was growing. From the balcony they could see flags blossoming everywhere. New institutions were feverishly being set up and on the avenue official cavalcades drove back and forth.

It was in the middle of a cockroach hunt, on 30th June, that an invitation arrived to attend the official banquet and Independence ceremonies in the *Palais de la Nation*.

Irène Laure had come for these historic days to join a group of about twenty men from Caux who were already there. The Congolese delegates to the Round Table talks in Brussels had asked the help of Moral Re-Armament to prevent their country from exploding into violence at the very moment of its birth. They set such store by this message of unity that in the heat of the preparations, as the government was with difficulty being formed, one or other of the new ministers would come each day to talk—or to be silent—with the guests from Caux. Four days away from the transfer of power, Patrice Lumumba came with nineteen of his brand new cabinet.

Alongside the French Socialist, the heterogeneous group included Blacks and Whites from South Africa, two former members of the Mau-Mau uprising and a white farmer from Kenya, three young American brothers with a genius for putting ideas into song, several Swiss and a Nigerian.

The day after the official reception, they had a surprise visit from a man Irène Laure and her companions had met several times before. Jean Bolikango was the chief of the great Bangala tribe. Everyone had been expecting him to be President or to have one of the key ministries. But he had been outmanoeuvred by pressure and intrigue and at Independence found himself, along with his tribe, forced into the background.

In a trice the table was laid with ill-assorted cutlery and fish was sizzling in the minute frying-pan.

'Why did you come and see me on Sunday?' Bolikango wanted to know. 'What made you come and find me in my hide-out? I was surrounded by my men who were desperate for revenge. We were ready to set fire to the whole town. I was about to make the fatal decision.'

Sitting round the table on improvised chairs, they hung on his every word and the fish was forgotten.

'Your coming and what you said made me prevent bloodshed. Your visit reawakened my conscience and now I don't think about my defeat any more.'

There was a remarkable similarity between the Bangala chief's response to his overthrow and Irène Laure's about-turn towards Germany thirteen years before. The pain of being accused of weakness, even betrayal, by close comrades was only too familiar to Bolikango, who for four days had been struggling to calm the angry spirits around him and prevent bitterness from destroying the country.

When he left to hurry back to his men, Bolikango had discovered that the voice in the silence, which prompted four strangers to ferret him out in his den one morning, was a force he could count on; in the weeks to come he would need it.

'Yes,' said Irène Laure to herself, in that long night of 7th July, 'a force which stands when everything is collapsing around us.'

Shortly before, when appeals on the radio had sent the whites scurrying to the Embassy in general panic, the group from Caux had obeyed instructions. Then they realised that any evacuation would take hours and they went back to the apartment to wait, to think and maybe even to sleep.

On her balcony, Irène Laure felt a surprising calm, a sense of being in the right place and that no event, however disastrous, could take from her that one essential—inner direction.

The short-lived dawn burst suddenly into day. Across the street the central post office remained shuttered. Neither telex nor telephone was operating during the crisis.

Clatterings on the landing: a family fleeing the countryside had arrived in the next-door apartment, the children still in their pyjamas and wide-eyed with fright.

Outside, lorryloads of armed men, jeeps and ambulances drove to and fro. Soldiers were stopping cars belonging to whites. By one of those curious twists of history, it was the two former Mau-Mau men who went shopping and brought back bread for Irène Laure and her companions, and also for the Belgians sheltering indoors.

It was a grim morning, and it heralded strange days for Irène Laure. As events made and unmade themselves and she was stuck on her eighth floor, she discovered that one did not necessarily need to be where the action was, but that one could also be a revolutionary on a balcony: if you couldn't go to people, lo and behold, they came to you.

Go or stay? Stay or go? Each time the balance seemed to lean towards leaving, someone would turn up who needed help to refind perspective or inner direction.

Unexpectedly on 12th July, a request came to the apartment from the Minister of Information, Anicet Kashamura: could they give a series of radio broadcasts which would help to establish calm?

The Minister came in person to take the group to the studios: 'We are so grateful that you have stayed on with us at the risk of your lives.'

On the 13th, as the sun was sinking behind the city, Irène Laure perched on the corner of the table from where she could both survey the avenue and hear the radio around which everyone was clustered.

'In spite of the difficult situation,' said the announcer, 'your friends from Moral Re-Armament, no, our friends from Moral Re-Armament, are not abandoning us. You will hear them every day; they are staying to help us build a strong and united country.'

From then on, morning and evening, just after the news, came the programme *There is an answer to crisis.* The letters of gratitude poured in, more than three thousand of them—a heartfelt cry from the whole country.

Visitors multiplied: Belgians torn apart by the situation and seeking to find where their duty lay, soldiers of the United Nations' forces who did not understand the ideological struggle, Congolese in search of new ways.

The United Nations troops brought an easing of tension in the streets but in the government the battle between ideologies grew more intense with each passing day.

On 20th July, without any warning, the Moral Re-Armament programme on the radio was replaced with a virulent speech by Madame Andrée Blouin, a Guinean much talked of since Independence, private secretary to the deputy Prime Minister, Antoine Gizenga, and well on the way to becoming the *éminence grise* of the government. In her broadcast she preached an 'African moral re-armament' based on solidarity among the oppressed and hatred of the whites.

One week later, *There is an answer to crisis* was taken off the air for good on the insistence of Andrée Blouin: the last straw had been the mention of a minister influenced by his Communist mistress. The story—a true one—referred to Japan. The broadcasts were not to resume until October, after the reversal of the political situation and the expulsion of Soviet advisers.

But on 20th July, another door opened.

The bell reverberated through the silent apartment; it was the door-bell of the servants' entrance. Consternation! No one used that staircase any more and all the suitcases and boxes had been piled against the back door. They were hastily taken down, while the bell rang impatiently.

'Ah, Madame Laure, we have found you at last!' exclaimed an imposing stranger. 'I am Mbengi Julienne, President of the women of Fabako.* I hear your broadcasts

*Women's section of President Kasavubu's Abako Party

every day on the national radio. What can I do for my women? Will you help me?'

She came in, stepping over the suitcases and settled down to make friends with the help of the secretary who translated volubly from Kikongo into French.

There was instant recognition—and how could it not be so, when they shared a compassion for women and children and a will to bring them out of misery and war? An appointment was made for calmer days, to show Moral Re-Armament films to the women of Fabako—who numbered two hundred and fifty thousand.

Almost every day they were in contact. Once, it was a feast in the African quarter, to which Madame Mbengi herself led her guests through interminable streets where there was not a white man to be seen, much less a white woman. Here and there a hostile gesture, but nearby a voice called out, 'Hallo, Madame Laure!'

Or else it was invitations to meetings at the headquarters of Fabako or at the Social Centre. At other times it was one or two women bringing a few oranges, asking questions and wanting to take away bits of paper on which they wrote: absolute honesty, absolute purity, absolute unselfishness, absolute love.

Film showings were organised in the flat: silent and serious the women would arrive, babies on their backs, their hands full of bananas and vegetables. There were films out of doors too, at the risk of having to break up the session when a curfew was declared.

Meanwhile Irène Laure could usually be found on her balcony. The cockroach-ridden flat had become a home full of life. Symbolic of the new era was the back door, which had only been used that one last time. The front staircase, formerly for whites only, was open to everyone.

For Irène Laure the family was one, embracing Mbengi

Julienne and her two hundred and fifty thousand women, her Belgian hostess of the first day who had become a dear friend, along with her own tenth grandchild, whose arrival she had heard about in the middle of the troubles, and Victor at home, so far and yet so near on this 12th August, their fortieth wedding anniversary.

The big red moon was there again, keeping count of the weeks that had passed. Was it mocking this revolutionary on her balcony? Or had it observed the power of silence initiating a revolution beyond violence more enduring than a moon?

Speaking on Radio Zaïre

What a price we paid in France for our liberation! How we suffered for it! At the end of 1944, we were free of the Germans, but what about liberation from the French? Victory was tainted with hatred, resentments, personal revenge. The freedom we had so greatly desired was a lie because there was no freedom in people's hearts.

One day Frank Buchman asked me, 'What kind of unity do you want for Europe?' It was a shock, because I realised for the first time in my life that, although I had always talked of peace and freedom, the deep hatred I held against the Germans would one day destroy the future of the grandchildren I loved.

I asked forgiveness for my hatred. That set my heart free from the mire of bitterness. I became a free woman, free to fulfil what is the role of every woman, every mother, every grandmother: to play a part in the enormous task of remaking the world through people.

Comrade Ima

'Madame Laure, how do you perceive Marxism and Communism and their long-term aims?'

Madame Kasavubu, wife of the President of Zaïre, had invited Irène Laure to visit her. The President joined them in the salon to put the question which was uppermost in his mind. It was just after three o'clock. At ten minutes to four, somebody put his head round the door to remind the President that he had an appointment.

'Oh, it'll be all right for another half hour. Tell them to wait!'

It was a quarter past four when the conversation finally drew to an end. The President and Madame Kasavubu waved from the doorstep until Irène Laure's car had rounded the lawn, just missing two or three Tibetan goats, and disappeared between the sentries guarding the gate.

Years later, in April 1974, the Prime Minister of another young African state, Swaziland, was to ask Irène Laure the same question.

This time it was in public, in the gleaming new Parliament buildings. The Prime Minister had just oulined his programme. He turned to Irène Laure:

'We would like you, as a grandmother and as a Socialist, to advise us about the kind of Socialism we should choose for the country we are building. So many brands of

Socialism are offered to us, and versions of democracy, too. The English tell us they have the best model. The Russians offer us their kind of democracy. What should we choose between all these ideologies?'

'For me,' she replied, 'the one and only formula for true world Socialism is on the basis of a transformation in human nature. Without healing hatred, Socialism will never become a reality.'

Another question, more personal this one, was put to her three times during a short stay in Laos in 1973, by the Prime Minister, by a General and by an Ambassador:

'Can a Socialist change?'

And Irène Laure, who believed in deeds and not in words and had a horror of talking about herself, had no choice but to tell and tell again the story of what she had experienced. For these questions were genuine, often anguished, and they had to be answered.

Conscious of the perspective and the understanding which the numerous contacts on her journeys had given her, she fought to the last ounce of her strength to help all those she met to understand the ideological stakes; in particular and faithfully, she did so with those who had been her colleagues in political life.

An example of this was a journey in August 1959 when she criss-crossed Europe with Mrs Shidzue Kato, member of the Japanese Senate Foreign Affairs Commission, and twelve political and trades union leaders from Japan. They expressed the spirit of their undertaking in a common declaration:

'To fulfil our Socialist mission we must learn to change people. If we do not learn to cure people's selfishness, Socialism will fail and we will follow the path of division and corruption.'

'Peaceful co-existence' was at that time in full swing,

offered to the Western world by Krushchev with an explosion of laughter or a bang of his shoe. Europe, especially northern Europe, hesitated between the apple of temptation and the apple of discord.... 'It took the Japanese to tell us the truth!' exclaimed one of the Socialists they visited.

Irène Laure must have felt the urgency of these contacts to make this record number of flights in such a few days, and at sixty years old, when she dreaded every departure from home.

The frontier-hopping did not take her to Rome this time; from Paris the Japanese went home via the North Pole, while Irène Laure paused for breath.

However she did not for a moment forget her neighbour, Italy, her father's homeland. Victor and Irène Laure had lost count of their trips to Italy. Whenever their travels took them to Rome they used to visit Giuseppe Saragat, whom they had known, poor and exiled, in Marseilles and who was to become President of the Republic in 1964. Remembering Giuseppina Saragat's fondness for *flageolets* from the Midi (a kind of kidney bean), Irène Laure always used to bring her a big bag of them, stowed away in their luggage.

One summer a man arrived in Caux claiming to be a converted Communist. He immediately made friends with the German workers who were there, several of whom had been expelled from the Communist Party because of their links with Caux. He offered his help to the trades unionists and workers. The work must be structured, he said, a file of contacts established; the Left must be regrouped.

Irène Laure shook her head.

'I will never betray the working class,' she explained to those who were attempting to establish a 'Left Wing' of Caux, 'because they are the people who suffer and they are

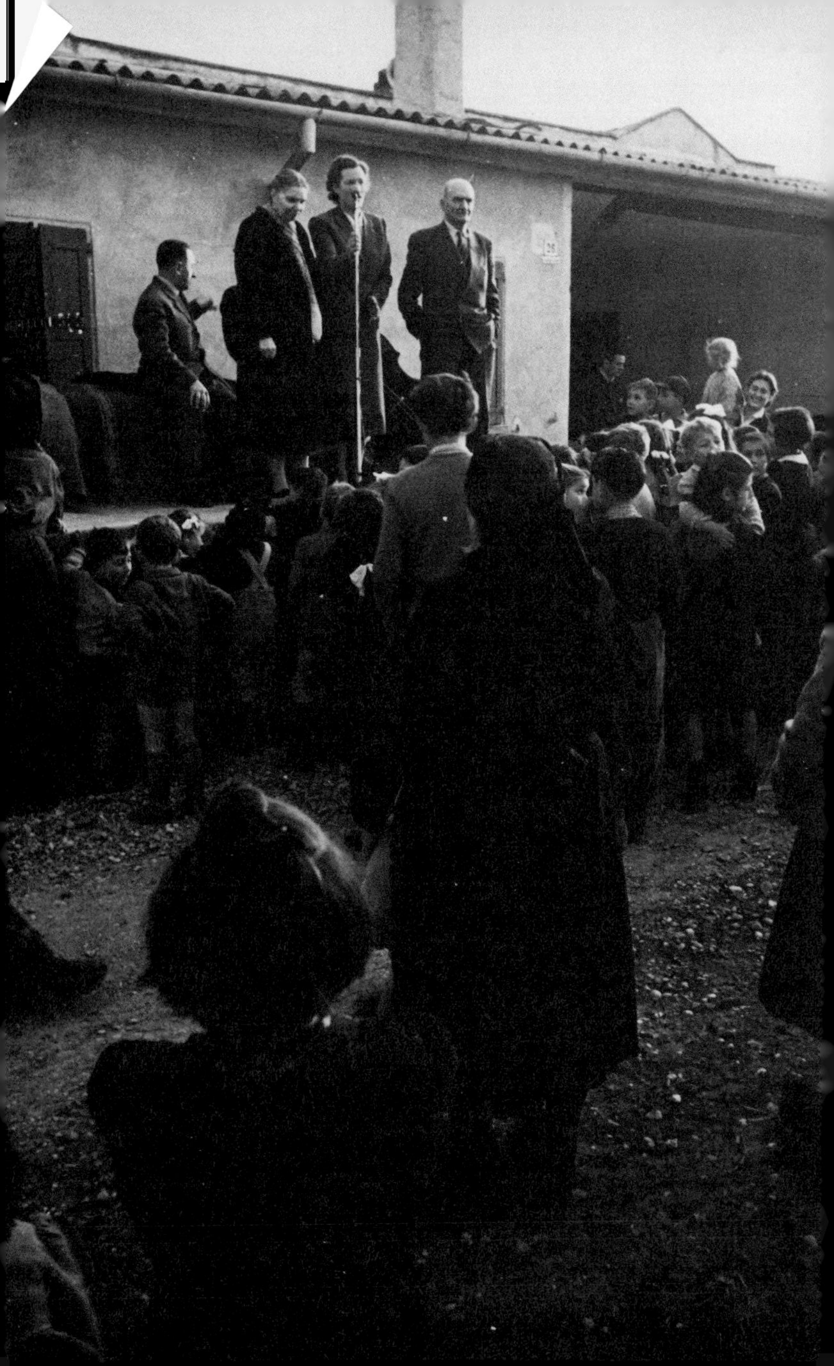

often the strength of a country. But I know that I serve the working class better by what we are doing than by waging the class war.'

Since the change in her attitude towards Germany, she had enlarged her aspirations to include the whole of humanity. She had pushed back the frontiers of Socialism. The stuff of which barriers are made was no longer even part of her. A 'workers' moral re-armament' seemed as far-fetched to her as the 'African moral re-armament' that Andrée Blouin had tried to launch on the radio in the summer of Zaïre's Independence. So the 'Left Wing' of Caux was a flop and its organiser disappeared the way he had come.

There was another kind of barrier which Irène Laure regarded as non-existent: language. In forty years of international contacts she had only French in which to express her ideas, but there always seemed to be someone to relay them into Kikongo, German or Japanese.

So it was that often, concealed behind Irène Laure— ill-concealed, for she was of imposing stature—was Princess Ima Lieven. She was so discreet that one would have thought her timid, this woman who had saved innumerable Resistants and Jews during the Occupation. She translated tirelessly, without ever putting herself forward, and Irène Laure often had to drag her out of the shadows to stand beside her.

After a pampered childhood in the castle which Catherine the Great had given to her ancestors in the Baltic state of Courland, Ima Lieven was caught in the upheaval of the revolution, escaping miraculously with her life on several occasions. Then, in Paris, she shared the fate of so many refugees, eking out a living from scant employment.

Torviscosa, in Trieste province

It was rare for her to recall the past and her distant homeland, still so dear to her. But sometimes she would add her own word to those she had so faithfully translated:

'I had always thought we were the martyrs of the revolution, the victims of events. It's not true. We were responsible for them. A privileged class which refuses to devote its energy and resources to the moral re-armament of the world condemns itself to the anger of the under-privileged.'

She translated for Irène Laure and she also acted as chauffeur in her black Citroën.

Here they were, once again, in the North. Victor Provo, Mayor of Roubaix, was on the phone. He had sat with Irène Laure on the executive committee of the Socialist Party and was inviting her to lunch:

'Do you have a driver?'

'Yes, I've someone who'll bring me.'

'Fine, we'll all have lunch together.'

It was a lively occasion. Provo held forth with vigour on the political situation and turned to 'the driver'.

'Wouldn't you agree, Comrade Ima?'

Comrade Ima she was and Comrade Ima she remained. Factory girls might dream of Cinderella becoming a princess. A Comrade Princess brought to life today that world family Irène Laure dreamed of for tomorrow.

The workers and young people in the parts of Asia, Africa and Latin America where I have been are fascinated by Socialism. For them it means a hope that things are going to change. How can we ensure that it is not a vain hope?

At a time when Socialists in Europe present a picture of division, where is the strength and unity of the Left? In the past our excuse was that we had our own struggles and our own needs – and then, India was so far away! But look at the speed of travel today and the amazing pace of modernisation. Isn't it the bold and exciting task of every Socialist to put everything into bringing an end, once and for all, to such human misery?

Without Socialism nothing of any scale or permanence will be done. I believe with all my heart in Socialism. It is inevitable, it is on the march. But Socialism without absolutely clear moral standards will destroy the world. We don't live our Socialism: there is pettiness, rivalry, sectarianism, a slide in morals and revolutionary discipline, the selfishness of refusing responsibility for the future. Let us stop bluffing about Socialism and start living it.

Answering the needs of these great continents is an enormous undertaking, but a thrilling one. Could it be that some Socialists in Europe are afraid to take it on? If so, they are not Socialists. Because Socialism demands that we give everything for a cause we believe to be right. And then our time, our money, our thinking and our families are mobilised in the task.

Tour of Japanese Socialists in Europe

P R O G R A M M E

*****

Tuesday 24th August 1959: BERLIN

- Television interview
- Reception by Willy Brandt, Socialist Mayor.
- Dinner organised by Ernst Scharnowski, President of the DGB (German Trades Union Confederation) Berlin Region.

Wednesday 25th August: BONN

- Press conference
- Dinner with Gerhard Schröder, Minister of the Interior, and Hans-Joachim von Merkatz, Minister for Relations with the Länder.

Thursday 26th and Friday 27th August: LONDON

- Meet Hugh Gaitskell, Leader of the Opposition Labour Party.
- Lunch with bankers and shipbuilders.
- Public meeting in East London.

Saturday 28th August: GLASGOW

- Press conference
- Dinner arranged by John McGovern, Labour Member of Parliament.
- Public meeting.

Tuesday 31st August: BERNE

- Lunch with trades unionists
- Discussion with Paul Chaudet, President of the Swiss Confederation.

Wednesday 1st September: COPENHAGEN

- Meet H-C Hansen, Socialist Prime Minister and Boerge Schmidt, Chairman of the Copenhagen Socialist Party.
- Press conference.

Thursday 2nd September: STOCKHOLM

- Breakfast with Arne Geijer, President of the Swedish Trades Unions and President of the ICFTU.
- Lunch with Patrik Svensson, President of the Parliament.
- Reception by Tage Erlander, Socialist Prime Minister.

Friday 3rd September: OSLO

- Discussion with Einar Gerhardsen, Socialist Prime Minister.
- Lunch with Rolf Stranger, Mayor of Oslo.
- Radio interview.

Saturday 4th September: HELSINKI

- Meet V-J Sukselainen, Socialist Prime Minister, Vaino Tanner, Chairman of the Socialist Party and Heikki Päiviö Hosia, Minister of Education.

Sunday 5th September: STOCKHOLM

- Public meeting.

Monday 6th and Tuesday 7th September: THE HAGUE

- Meet J-B De Quay, Prime Minister
- Reception by the President of the Senate, J-A Jonkman (interned in Japanese prison camps during the war).
- Press conference.

Wednesday 8th September: PARIS

- Breakfast with Gabriel Marcel.
- Meet Edmond Michelet, Minister of Justice.
- Discussion with Guy Mollet, General Secretary of the SFIO (Section Française de l'Internationale Ouvrière), Ernest Cazelles, Assistant General Secretary, and Charles Pot, head of the press department.

With Mrs Shidzue Kato, member of the Foreign Affairs Committee of the Japanese Senate, and the delegation

1974
Pretoria

'I thought I knew a good deal, but since I arrived in South Africa I've had to learn more every day.'

It was 1974. Irène Laure was seventy-five and she was treading South African soil for the first time.

'You'll see, when you leave, your ideas about our country may be even less clear than when you came!'

Foresight with a touch of Afrikaans humour and a great deal of wisdom. South Africa is surely the subject *par excellence* about which Europeans think they know, and hold forth (sometimes without ever having listened to South Africans).

The man talking to Irène Laure was Arthur Grobbelaar, General Secretary of TUCSA, at that time comprising sixty-nine trades unions, White, Coloured, Asian and mixed. The Black associations were not counted in this figure as at that time they had no official status—which did not prevent Grobbelaar from supporting every attempt by Blacks to form themselves into unions. 'When there are enough, the government will be obliged to recognise them,' he said.

Irène Laure had not had any intention of trotting off to South Africa. But an invitation had arrived. George Daneel, a minister of the powerful Dutch Reformed Church and former member of its Synod, Cornelius

Marivate, Professor of African languages at the University of South Africa, and others she had met in Caux, had embarked on an impossible undertaking: an inter-racial conference in Pretoria, bastion of apartheid.

But how could she even think of joining them, when Saturday, 6th April was the wedding day of the first of her grandchildren, Yves? The family needed to gather around her all the more now that Victor's place was empty; empty since that evening just after Christmas, 1960, when he had died in the arms of his Irène.

Then, on the eve of the wedding, everything was turned upside down. Irène Laure could not resist her inner prompting; she could no longer refuse these courageous men. Saturday belonged wholly to her family. But at midnight, her ears buzzing and her heart satisfied, she was back at *La Sarine* and beginning to pack. Sunday, the train for Paris and first thing on Monday, the necessary visit to the Embassy, where, fortunately, the formalities were speedily completed: in ten minutes the visa was in her passport.

In Pretoria the three hundred conference participants were staying at the Burgers Park Hotel, with the permission of the Minister of the Interior, for it was not everywhere that Black, Coloured, Asian and White South Africans and their guests from Brazil, Europe and Australia could all stay under the same roof. How the Kenyans and Nigerians persuaded their governments to allow them to visit South Africa was another wonder. Indeed, one might well ask whether there was anything about this conference that was not miraculous.

Irène Laure breezed in on Tuesday, just in time for the opening. A gala evening, formal dress—you had to pinch yourself to believe it. For Irène Laure, no problem about what to wear: out of her suitcase came the usual little cotton dress, grey, with the smartening touch of a white jabot. She was expected for the inaugural dinner at the top table, presided over by the Mayor of Pretoria. There she found George Daneel, Cornelius Marivate, all the people whose invitation she had been unable to resist.

Coaches had been hired to take the three hundred participants through the green jacaranda-lined streets, up to the hill on which stood the University of South Africa. All week the startled pedestrians caught fleeting glimpses of a society without segregation.

When Irène Laure reached the magnificent amphitheatre, it was packed to the last seat with a thousand people. 'Unbelievable' was the word which sprang to mind at the sight of this multi-racial audience and it recurred throughout the evening as Blacks, Whites, Coloureds and Indians all spoke from the platform. She spoke, too, diffidently at first and then quickly fired by the strength of her conviction.

An unbelievable evening indeed, which opened the door to six days of dialogue, often painful, sometimes difficult, sometimes laughter-filled, but resolutely oriented towards that profound transformation which could yet break the chain reaction of fear and hate.

Irène Laure spent a memorable evening with a leader of the Garment Workers' Union, a Coloured woman, in her home. Another in the Black township of Soweto, on the outskirts of Johannesburg, where she was invited by two young women in domestic service. She marvelled at the patch of garden which each family tended with such loving pride and the immaculate little houses—and yet how could she avoid comparing them with the quality of the White and even the Coloured homes? The Blacks were not allowed to own even these small plots. Those women had a two-hour journey to work every morning, with no hope of ever being allowed to live nearer at hand.

For Irène Laure, every injustice was intolerable. At the age of five, she had responded with direct action: Papa's socks. When the taxi-driver refused to let her travel with a Black companion, she was within inches of making a scene. She gritted her teeth and restrained herself out of respect for a Black politician with whom she had dined the first evening. 'Violence as a means of change,' he said, 'is an instrument of despair. A short-term solution which in fact resolves nothing. You in Europe know that better than anyone. You have had two world wars and what have they changed? For us, any solution must come through a change in ourselves, because this sort of change will make friends out of all the citizens of South Africa, while violence will only leave us a long inheritance of hatred.'

Among the courageous Afrikaners she met during those days, there was one whose words went straight to her heart.

'We did not choose our colour,' he said, 'but we can choose what our contribution will be to the future of the children of this country.'

Many were the Blacks and Whites who saw in the Pretoria conference a sign of the country's will towards change. For them, there was no going back. For Irène Laure, who had staked everything on changing society through a transformation in people, the challenge was to hold fast to that faith, especially when it required such courage.

'Since it was possible for you and the Germans,' several people said to her, 'why not for us?'

So Irène Laure listened. She denied herself the easy option of taking sides. She listened and in her presence no one felt either judged or condemned.

When she spoke, it was to share the hope she had found throught the change in herself and the changes of which she had been a privileged witness for so many years. In her mind, apologising was not a gesture of goodwill but a bold and courageous step which broke the chain of hate and could in record time make possible what looked like impossible solutions.

'We in the Republic of South Africa are late starters on this road of building a fear-free, hate-free, greed-free world,' they said, 'but this doesn't mean we shall not reach the finishing post.'

1976
Israel

Golda Meir's little office was unpretentious. A table, three, four chairs, not even any curtains. All fire, this mother of the nation was also all simplicity.

'I know you,' she said at once to Irène Laure.

From where, who could tell. She could have heard, she could have read—what? There was no doubt that she sympathised.

'You've only been a Socialist since you were sixteen,' she commented. 'I began at six and in Russia, at that.'

A common passion united the two women: concern for the kind of world that future generations would know.

'I never allowed my son or my grandchildren to play with guns when they were small. Now, I calculate that for the next twelve years without a break I'll have at least one grandson bearing arms....'

Irène Laure spoke of the war and the Resistance, of Louis. Like those who have suffered much, Golda Meir knew how to listen with her heart.

'One cannot forget,' said Irène Laure, 'but one can forgive and ask forgiveness. Can you imagine what it was like for a French mother? Two hundred times I apologised, in public, for my hatred, because I had willed the bombs to destroy the German people. Even if I think that I am only ten per cent in the wrong, I must make the first step and take responsibility for my ten per cent.'

Golda Meir did not answer. In the corridors of power a change of heart and forgiveness are not often reckoned with. It took a little time for the ideas to sink in.

When she came to herself, it was to ask her secretary to bring them cups of tea.

Golda Meir was a weary woman. She was recovering slowly from an operation. She had resigned from office two years before, but not a day went by without a member of the government or some official coming to ask her advice.

'How encouraging it is,' she sighed, 'to meet someone who hasn't given up the fight.'

'One must never give up hope,' replied Irène Laure.

'Oh, you're right, we must go on hoping in spite of everything, even if we don't see any results. Thank you for coming to see me, it is a great honour.'

Brother Joseph's little grey Citroën bounced Irène Laure over the cobbles and climbed gamely to the top of the hill. As far as the eye could see, Jerusalem sparkled in the sunlight. A city which had been only a name sprang to life. The centuries unfolded; here the book of history was open on every page at once.

On one page Irène Laure saw Jewish mothers holding out their babies to her, the day before a journey from which there would be no return, the journey to the concentration camps. How many times had she hidden these hunted children in the generous folds of her black coat?

Behind all the little cupolas, amidst the harmony of golden stone or in towering sky-scrapers, were the children she had rescued thirty years before raising their own families, she wondered, and was it for war or for peace?

Like the echo of too much suffering—undergone, inflicted, repaid, what did it matter? Tears all taste the same—a conviction rose to her lips: Jerusalem, city of reconciliation.

It was only December. Winter had not yet run its course. A jaunty little bird was hiding in the cypress beside her. Strain her eyes as she might, he was invisible. But his trills danced out of the dark branches in irresistible cascades. No, one must never lose hope.

I got rid of my hatred. I had a great hatred of the Germans. Facing facts, I was right. I suffered a lot from the war and I hardened myself so I should never weep again. Even when I heard one of my sons had been tortured, I did not weep. I hardened my heart and said, 'They'll pay for it.' They did pay–but I felt ashamed and I asked their forgiveness, because no nation makes war alone.

The most difficult thing for the French is to face that France has been wrong, because we daren't admit that France might be wrong. I asked forgiveness for myself and for the mistakes France had made. It is hard, very hard, but if you do that then you know complete freedom and you can contribute to the freedom and peace of the world.

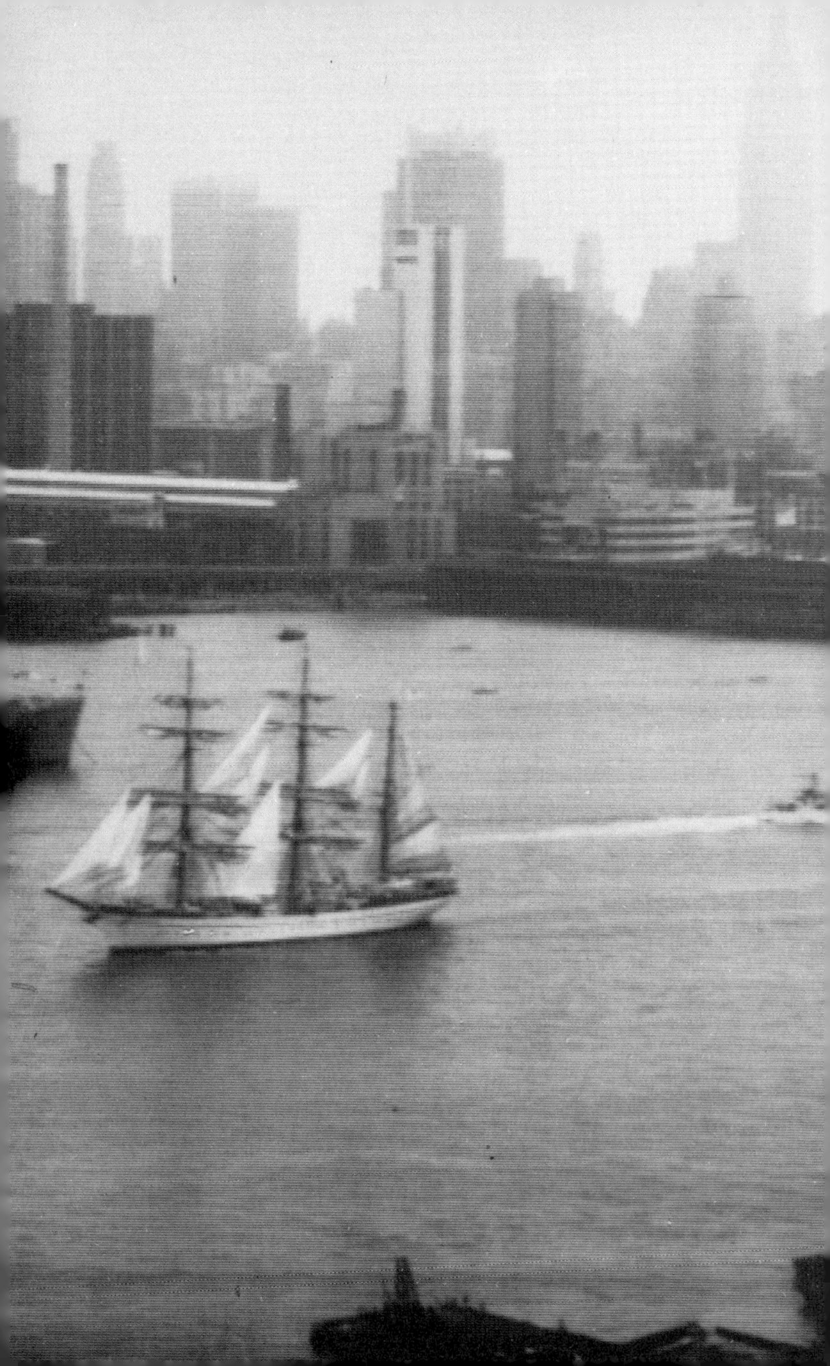

1976

Bicentennial

1976 saw Irène Laure in the United States for the fifteenth time. She had needed such persuasion to set foot in America at all; could she possibly have been seduced by these despicable capitalists?

Well, she loved them and what's more she believed in them, however often they might put their foot in it—rather like her own children and grandchildren, those precious Marseillais rogues.

From the start she was overwhelmed by American generosity. She never forgot the foodstuffs that had saved her own children's lives and the lives of so many children in Europe after the war.

Accustomed as she was to giving generous hospitality, she marvelled as much this time as on her first visit at the boundless welcome she encountered in American families. They asked you to make yourself at home—and they meant it.

Like all generosity, that of the USA can cause gritted teeth and misunderstandings. 'People have so misjudged America,' Irène Laure would say sometimes. So she went. And she kept on returning.

1976, two hundred years of history, which some scorned from the great heights of their millennia. But Irène Laure celebrated with all the enthusiasm of a child. If her legs baulked at following the historical parade in the streets of Washington, never mind; she spent the whole of the Fourth of July in front of the television, thrilling at the sight of the crowd moving as one.

The exuberance of these celebrations was a measure of the anguish which had turned the country in on itself since the tragedy of Vietnam and the trauma of Watergate. In New York, eight million people crowded the banks of the Hudson River to watch as sixteen tall ships from all over the world, majestic in full sail, passed before the Statue of Liberty. In Washington the procession relived in pageantry the history of America from the pioneers to the conquest of space. That inventive and generous spirit which had captured Irène Laure was given free rein. Also that faculty, so disconcerting to the Cartesian spirit, of not experimenting discreetly and in private, but of displaying all that one is, all one's discoveries, all one's inventions, even at the risk of losing face in the process.

At the front marched Vice-President Rockefeller and the Mayor—a black man—who had the rare good fortune of bearing the same name as the city he administered.

From time to time Irène Laure would run out on to the balcony to get the feel of the crowd. A loved one's birthday is always a cause for rejoicing. Flags slapped in the breeze, there was singing and high jinks and whistling at the rockets and fireworks.

This American visit lasted only a few weeks but it was filled. Journeys and meetings followed each other in quick succession. It amused her to calcuate that she had already been in thirty of the States of the Union. How many Americans could say as much? And whatever else, she was sure to find time to have a peep at Vermeer's 'The Girl with a Red Hat', a favourite picture in the National Gallery in Washington.

Back to Richmond, Virginia, where she had been in 1947. She was moved to revisit a big house surrounded with trees, the Chapin family home, which they had put at the disposal of Moral Re-Armament. William Chapin had financed the visit of the first Germans to Caux by selling a life insurance policy. It might have seemed rash then to invest in European reconciliation but it had proved to be a good investment. And thirty years later Mr. Chapin was still going strong and, having moved out of his home, was now living in a caravan on his son's ranch.

The variety of people she met reflected the diversity of the pioneers, assimilated into one country. There were glass-blowers in a craft village, leaders of the Puerto Rican community, native American Indians, trades unionists and dockers, young people, masses of young people, and Pan-Am employees, old friends from Miami, 1952.

And she never tired of these entire suburbs without a hedge or a fence to divide one garden from another: that open, hospitable spirit again. Even the cemetery was not shut away.

She met families where they did not only forage for themselves in the fridge. In one place, a biologist—and sometime organist—who loved her work but had given it up for a few years because she saw that her presence at home was important for the children. In another, parents who had got rid of their television set in order to find a more creative family life. Meals that had to simmer, home-made bread: a different America!

Before taking off for the Old World, one more sally, to Norfolk, Virginia, a hundred miles from Richmond. Gates, sentries, entry-passes; one did not just walk into a giant naval base, even if it was to lunch with the Commandant of the Armed Forces' Staff College.

In Admiral Denton's office a table was laid. The damask

cloth with its fleur-de-lys design was put out specially by Jane Denton in honour of the French guest, a gesture which went straight to Irène Laure's heart.

Scarcely were the introductions made before the Admiral was asking his first question: 'I am told that your son was tortured during the war. What has become of him since?'

Irène Laure knew that Denton had been a prisoner of the North Vietnamese for seven years, of which four were in solitary confinement, and that he had been tortured several times. His talks with his gaolers had left him with an intense concern for the worlds behind the bamboo and iron curtains.

In this conversation he was searching. Could that experience of reconciliation of which Irène Laure had been a part, and which had now gone down in history, hold a key to the survival of today's world?

For a father of seven, the future could not be in the abstract. So they had no difficulty in understanding one another; lunch had to be extended, upsetting the Admiral's schedule in very un-naval fashion.

'I beg you,' was Irène Laure's call to America, 'have the courage to do something great, something really great.'

I have seen two wars and twice I have seen the Americans come to our aid. I know the price they paid for our senseless European quarrels. No statistics or expressions of gratitude can ever set a true value on it. That would be impossible. Oh, I am not saying the Americans are always right. Oh no! But in my view, the price they paid can never be calculated.

And of course, they have given still more through that great American, Frank Buchman. It is not a question of counting up how many died. Nor can we count how many people came to a faith in Jesus Christ through Frank Buchman-like my husband and myself, our friends Bladeck and Kurowski from the Ruhr in Germany and so many others-but I should like you to understand what Frank Buchman gave the world in terms of hope. He showed us a philosophy of life which is able to transform situations and perhaps-I say perhaps-lead to peace.

1983

Liverpool

'Would you mind turning off your machine for a moment, please?'

Somewhat taken aback, the journalist pressed the switch on his tape-recorder. Perhaps his questioning had been a bit too aggressive? He had to admit that in order to liven up his interview for Radio Merseyside, he had tried to corner Irène Laure by asking her loaded questions about the Common Market.

He had not reckoned that although she might be past her three score years and ten, she was not going to let herself be cornered. Indeed with her, an interviewer stood a good chance of being interviewed himself—as he was soon to find out. Once rid of the 'machine', Irène Laure fixed him with her clear gaze and said,'As a great-grandmother, I have a question to ask you: when you were young, weren't you a scamp?'

The initiative had changed sides. An hour later the journalist departed with a tape on Europe ready for transmission, the man himself with food for thought.

Always ready for new experiences, Irène Laure found herself at lunchtime at the top of a tower with her nose to a picture window, gazing at a panorama of the city unfolding as the restaurant turned slowly on its axis. Her heart beat for the port and the docks, but what delighted her in this industrial metropolis, whose image abroad is so often associated with violence, was the street linking the two cathedrals.

At the southern end, austere, superb with its Gothic arches and rosy sandstone, the Anglican cathedral. At the northern end, a huge tepee of glass and concrete, the Catholic cathedral, its stained-glass tower throwing rainbows over the city.

The street between them is called Hope Street.

Hope for tomorrow or the day after, she thought, as she looked at the once well-kept streets now left to decay, and the young unemployed walking the pavements, or as she read the tourist brochure advising the precautions to be taken against crime.

Hope for today as she talked to members of the municipal council, to those in charge of the port, to African students at a hostel or to a youth group campaigning for the Third World.

Liverpool touched Irène Laure with memories. She discovered that the nun showing her round the Cathedral of Christ the King had been in concentration camp with Geneviève Anthonioz-de Gaulle. When she heard the story of the pilgrimage of the German miners to Mont Valérien, the nun wept.

Another glimpse of the past: the French consul had been posted to Rio de Janeiro in the fifties, and had helped Louis in his epic beginnings in Brazil.

In each of her encounters through these days, there was one subject which Irène Laure never lost from sight. For her the European situation was as serious in 1983 as after the war. It was with the longing to consolidate the bases of European unity that she had crossed the Channel for the third time in eighteen months.

'In order to build Europe,' she said, '—and when I say

Europe I always include Great Britain—what is lacking? The essential: honesty, sincerity between countries, and not only at the level of the politicians.'

One day she discovered—yet another of those coincidences which no longer even surprised her—that three hours' drive away, in a small Welsh town, there was to be a coffee evening about Europe to raise money for a film about her life and her contribution to Franco-German reconciliation. She didn't think twice. Off to Wales, where the organisers of the gathering had the surprise of their lives to see the 'subject' of their coffee evening appear in the flesh.

'Tonight we've heard of a different side of Europe from the one you usually get from the press and politicians,' said a Welsh Member of the European Parliament in conclusion, quite forgetting that she too was a politician.

For Irène Laure herself, Europe was not a political issue but one of civilisation and values. And when it came to a battle, and an important battle at that, should one not gamble on the best of Britain?

'When the British lion once gets his teeth into something,' said Irène Laure with a twinkle, 'he doesn't let go until he's won!'

The longer I live the more I realise that unity between Britain and France is vital for the world. The more links we form, the better. Whether I shall ever succeed, I do not know, but I should very much like to learn a little English—a curious language, don't you think? But I like hearing it.

Having lived through two wars, I know it is essential to create a united Europe—not just a unity of heart and mind but also in economic terms.

I am not always goodnatured, you see. For instance, when I see Britain causing difficulties over lamb, I say to myself, 'To hell with Britain!' We are so different in character – I mean the French and the English. During the war there was de Gaulle and there was Mr Churchill. They were hopeless when they got together, those two. Churchill once said that de Gaulle was his thorn in the flesh, but he added, 'If I were in his position I should do the same.' Why is it that in times of danger we do our utmost to get on with one another? Can we not do our utmost in peacetime to find the best way forward? It would be such an encouragement for other nations, just as it was in Caux when reconciliation began with the Germans.

1983
Spring

A signpost on the road: Ravensbrück. Forty years on, the pain has not ebbed.

'No, you are not betraying those who died here. They died that life should go on. Forget, no. Forgive, yes, for hate will always bring war in its train.'

Once again, Irène Laure is on her travels. At home, the poppies are blooming. Here in Germany, she is back at the start of spring.

As she approaches eighty-five, it is not easy to leave home and Claude's attentive care, but Irène Laure does not believe in retirement when it comes to the world her descendants will inherit.

The Rhine sparkles, blue-green between the barges. The road caresses the foot of the Drachenfels—but of Siegfried or the dragon, no sign—through the trim village of Rhöndorf to the house with the roses. Konrad Adenauer no longer tends his precious rose-bushes in the terraced garden. The house is a museum now, crowded with anonymous visitors.

But Irène Laure is not a visitor. She is a daughter of the house, welcomed with open arms by Anneliese Poppinga.

Dr. Poppinga was Konrad Adenauer's secretary for enough years to know the gratitude he felt towards the French *résistante* who cut the cord of hatred between their two countries.

In the Chancellor's dining-room, glowing with polished furniture, they swap memories over cups of coffee.

Behind the ropes—the penalty of being a museum—the flow of visitors never dries up, and many a curious glance is directed at the happy faces around the table. The intoning of the guide drifts through from the sitting-room next door.

Adenauer, Schuman, Jean Monnet live again, while through the windows the friends catch glimpses of school groups going round the rose garden.

Then it's a whole gang of young men on military service, in their blue uniforms. There is an instant response from Anneliese Poppinga who rushes to open the big French windows and introduce Irène Laure to the young soldiers.

Caught short, Irène Laure searches for words. But there is no need to fear. She finds a couple of phrases on the rebellious daughter her parents had to handle, followed by, 'As for me, I love rascals,' and contact is established. The soldiers are spellbound.

'You see, Madame,' says one, in impeccable French, 'we are not soldiers for war but for peace.'

Berlin welcomes her next and for the eighth or ninth time, flaunting all the trappings of opulence.

On a hill at Grunewald, children just out of school shout happily as they chase one another. The trees there are less than forty years old. The children do not know that their roots are planted in millions of cubic metres of rubble collected by the women of Berlin, their own grandmothers, with their bare hands.

Today, misery lies elsewhere.

Among the young people with nothing to do, who dress their despair in trendy disguises and explode in almost daily demonstrations.

In the squatter-occupied buildings and the police sirens' refrain.

In the frenzy of consumerism unleashed in the shops.

In the bouquets of flowers reminding the Wall of its dead.

It is also among the Turkish immigrants, the doors of return and the doors of employment equally closed to them. And Irène Laure cannot leave Berlin without a visit to them.

On Peacock Island fifty teenagers from a Turkish school gather for a picnic. The girls pass round rice balls and aubergine fritters. Western one moment and a moment later drawing the traditional veil over their foreheads—like a sky hesitating between rain and shine.

A breeze ruffles the river towards the sinister Wall imprisoning it in the distance.

Translated into German by a teacher from Berlin who was badly wounded in the war and retranslated afterwards into Turkish, Irène Laure answers the questions of these young people who seem so disoriented. She speaks to them as if they were her own grandchildren and the brightness she unveils makes them forget the intermittent showers.

'I have never regretted anything in my life, but I do regret not being your age. What a wonderful task is awaiting you! I am not afraid of the future, I look forward to it.'

Another meeting with that friend from the early days, Ernst Scharnowski, just now depressed and discouraged. To him, too, Irène Laure says, 'No, I'm not afraid of the future, I'm looking forward to it!'

At *La Sarine,* she puts on her apron again and her flowery hat.

'Mami, will you tell us a story?'

'Oh yes, a story about when you were little.'

And, being Irène Laure, how can she refuse, even if she had planned to weed the border?

In La Ciotat, like everywhere else, a great-grandmother's stories are magical.

'When I was a little girl, knee high to a grasshopper, I had curly hair, with ringlets at the sides—just imagine!'

'Oh,' say the children, looking at the smooth white hair, carefully tied back.

'I had a dream. I dreamed about the world. The new world.'

'Wuff, wuff,' comments the loyal Jeff, who already knows the story and is dreaming of a world without ticks.

Irène Laure recalls her summers in Chamonix, the ponies Pompon and Bibi which she rode with her sister, the cook's biscuits, Papa's socks. She tells them about the war—as little as possible—and then.... but it would fill a whole book!

Cécile heaves a big sigh: 'Does it have a happy ending?'

'You know,' she says, thinking aloud, 'I find it hard to believe that all this happened to me.'

The sun-kissed little faces draw closer. Gilles, the youngest, clings to her skirt, winsome.

'But, Mami, why did you do all that?'

Should she say the 'for you' which flickers to life inside her?

'Do you know, I couldn't do otherwise.'

And in her clear eyes there is a twinkle.

Sources of Reference

Office universitaire de Recherche socialiste OURS, Paris (procès-verbaux du comité directeur de la SFIO 1945-1948)
Institut d'Histoire du Temps présent, Paris (résistance dans les Bouches du Rhône 1943-1945)
Archives Nationales (rapports préfectoraux des Bouches du Rhône 1943-1945)
Archive des Conférences de Caux 1947-1984
Archives de la Mairie de Chamonix
Archives des Bouches du Rhône à Marseille
Virginia State Library, Richmond, 1947-1948
Library of Congress, Washington (Manuscript Division 1947-1948)

André Sauvageot *Marseille dans la tourmente*, Ed. Ozanne 1949
Jean Lacouture *Léon Blum*, Seuil 1977
Jean Lacouture *Pierre Mendès France*, Seuil 1981
Christopher Sykes *Troubled Loyalty, a Biography of Adam von Trott*, Collins 1969
Silvain Reiner *Grand-mère Patrie*, Albin Michel 1980
Philippe Mottu *The Story of Caux from La Belle Epoque to Moral Re-Armament*, Grosvenor Books 1970
Robert Carmichael par lui-même, preface by Jean Rey, Ed. de Caux 1975
Charles Piguet and Michel Sentis *The World at the Turning*, Grosvenor Books, 1982
Plus décisif que la violence, presented by Gabriel Marcel, Plon 1971
Leif Hovelsen *Out of the Evil Night*, Blandford 1959

People consulted

Odette Naegler, secretary to Irène Laure at the SFIO from 1945 to 1948,
Simone Delsel who at that time ran the secretariat for Socialist (SFIO) Members of Parliament,
Jean Loup, Protestant pastor of Aubagne 1938—48,
Maurice Nosley, who first invited Irène Laure to the Caux conferences (and was shown the door!),
Angela Nosley, Françoise Caubel, Lucie Perrenoud and Marie-Claude Borel, who kept detailed diaries of their travels with Irène Laure,
and above all the daughters and sons of Victor and Irène Laure who, for the love of tomorrow, opened the door of their secret garden.

Speeches by Irène Laure

p 4   Dusseldorf: 19th January, 1949
p 13   La Ciotat: April, 1983
p 19   Caux: 13th July, 1953
p 26   Caux: 19th June, 1949
p 37   Caux: 15th July, 1969
p 42   Le Touquet: November, 1948
p 47   Lille: 1st December, 1951
p 52   Caux: September, 1949
p 53   Caux: 28th June, 1949
p 58   Caux: 4th October, 1953
p 65   Srinagar (Kashmir): 10th May, 1953
p 66   Caux: 15th July, 1959
p 72   Caux: 5th August, 1954
p 88   Caux: 5th August, 1954
p 98   Kinshasa: 15th July, 1960
p 105   Paris: 25th January, 1964
p 117   Caux: 14th July, 1953
p 123   London: 30th April, 1980
p 128   Tirley Garth: September, 1982

Photos

David Channer: Cover, pp 8, 25, 66
Jeremy McCabe: iii, 57, 84
Michael Blundell: 29, 46, 102
Arthur Strong: 30, 38, 51, 68, 71, 107
Laure family collection: 33, 89
Peter Sisam: 48
Ivor Sharp: 61
Robert Fleming: 76
Keystone: 118